Pete Aguereberry and the author George Pipkin at Harris-burg Flats in 1941.

Pete Aguereberry

Death Valley Prospector & Gold Miner

---

by George C. Pipkin

MURCHISON PUBLICATIONS
TRONA, CALIFORNIA 93562

FIRST EDITION 1971
SECOND EDITION 1982

ISBN 0-930704-11-8
LIBRARY OF CONGRESS CATALOG CARD NO. 81-84564

TYPOGRAPHICALLY DESIGNED AND SET ON THE LINOTYPE BY THE
SAGEBRUSH PRESS / MORONGO VALLEY, CALIF. 92256

DEDICATED TO:

MYRTLE EUNICE PIPKIN MURCHISON
—*my number one daughter!*

CONTENTS

		PAGE
	AUTHOR'S FOREWORD	9
I.	JOURNEY TO THE LAND OF PROMISE	15
II.	COURTING DISASTER	22
III.	THE LONELY TRAIL	30
IV.	A NEW BEGINNING	36
V.	LOVE GOES AGLIMMERING	40
VI.	GAMBLING FEVER	47
VII.	STALKED BY THE GRIM REAPER	54
VIII.	DEATH VALLEY SCOTTY	62
IX.	EUREKA!	69
X.	BALLARAT	79
XI.	HARRISBURG GOLD RUSH	84
XII.	SHATTERED DREAMS	91
XIII.	SKIDOO	97
XIV.	THE LYNCHING OF HOOTCH SIMPSON	103
XV.	CELEBRATIONS	115
XVI.	BEAR TALE	122
XVII.	SAM ADAMS	125
XVIII.	JEANE (JOHN) LEMOIGNE	133
XIX.	ARNAUD AGUEREBERRY	139
XX.	PETE'S LEGACY	144
	A FEW WORDS ABOUT THE AUTHOR	149
	INDEX	151
	MAP OF THE DEATH VALLEY REGION	159

22 PHOTOGRAPHIC ILLUSTRATIONS FOLLOW PAGE 96

AUTHOR'S FOREWORD

On the Wildrose cutoff to Death Valley through the rugged Panamint Mountains in Inyo County, California, and the Death Valley National Monument, there's a road sign pointing east that reads "Aguereberry Point - 6 miles". The point overlooking Death Valley was named in honor of the late Jean Pierre "Pete" Aguereberry.

Pete Aguereberry was a trail partner with Frank "Shorty" Harris, when he made a gold discovery on July 1, 1905.

The two men, both prospectors, were punching their burro trains westward through the Panamint Mountains over the old Blackwater Canyon Indian Trail. They had crossed Death Valley at night, coming from the Greenland Ranch (now Furnace Creek Ranch) and were headed for the town of Ballarat, a mining supply center in Panamint Valley. Pete's business in Ballarat was to pick up a money order at the post office from his grubstaking partners, Frank Flynn and Tom Kavanagh who lived in Goldfield, Nevada. Shorty was hurrying to Ballarat to celebrate the Fourth of July in the town's many saloons.

When the two men broke over the summit of the Panamints and started across the wide plateau, Pete's ever-alert eyes spied a promising outcropping near the trail. Pete asked Shorty to wait for him while he investigated the outcropping. But Shorty, a man in a hurry, said "Holy Smokes, Pete, Fourth of July! Let's get on to Ballarat!" He rode off and left Pete behind.

The first piece of rock Pete knocked from the ledge with his pick contained free gold. When he finally caught up with Shorty and showed him the gold in the rock, Shorty exclaimed, "Holy Smokes, Fourth of July, we're both rich!"

Shorty did not hold onto his riches long. As soon as his share of the claims were staked out and duly recorded, he sold them and went on a prolonged binge that lasted until he was flat broke.

Shorty was a playboy among the prospectors. He spent a lot of time in the mining camp saloons prospecting drinks out of those who would listen to him brag about what a great prospector the short man was, and about the great discoveries he had made.

But this is not a story about Shorty Harris, it is about Pete Aguereberry, who was the complete opposite of Shorty Harris. Being a French Basque, he was clean-cut, industrious, thrifty and close-mouthed. At one period in his life you will find he was suspicious of people and bank checks. There was the time that Pete sold his mine, the Eureka, to a San Francisco mining syndicate for $100,000 cash. When the syndicate executive and his lawyer showed up at the mine with a bill of sale for Pete to sign, along with a cashier's check for $100,000, Pete asked, "Where's the cash?" To which the executive answered, "Surely, Mr. Aguereberry, you wouldn't expect us to be lugging $100,000 in cash around in the wilds of Death Valley would you?" Pete refused to accept the check and the sale fell through.

As the story unfolds you will see how unscrupulous people, in the early days, took advantage of his inability to speak and understand their language. Sheepherding, working as a ranch hand, prospecting and mining offered him little opportunity to learn the English language. Eventually he did learn it, though it took several years and he did it the hard way. Naturally, he learned all the curse words first.

When I first met him in 1928 in Trona, he spoke fluent English with a slight accent and his penmanship was above average. In my files I have one of Pete Aguereberry's letters which he mailed to me from San Pedro on March 16, 1944. That letter was instrumental, in 1966, in having the United States Department of the Interior's Board of Geographic Names correct the spelling of Aguerreberry Point to Aguereberry. I had remembered that Pete once told me that the old-country spelling was Aguerreberry, but when he came to America and learned to write his name in English, he dropped the first "r" to shorten the name.

Pete hung onto his mine in Harrisburg Flat until the day he died. It was his home for 40 years. In later years, he only mined when in need of money for living expenses. He paid cash for everything he bought. Over the years, the mine became a tourist attraction. Pete never tired of guiding people through it and there was never a charge. Another of his greatest pleasures was taking people up to Aguereberry Point to share with them the spectacular view of Death Valley 6,279 feet below.

Long before Death Valley National Monument was established on February 11, 1933, Pete carved out a road by hand, using a pick, shovel, wheelbarrow and blasting powder, from his mine up to the Point, a distance of four and a half miles. When asked why he had expended so much of his time and hard labor building the road, his answer was simple—he merely wanted to share the wonderful view of Death Valley with others. There was never a toll charge.

When Pete made the original strike in 1905, it was the custom of the times for a trail partner to share equally in the discovery. So Shorty Harris got his share of the claims. Before the two men reached Ballarat, they had agreed to name the strike site "Harrisberry," but Shorty kept calling it "Harrisburg" and that's the name it bears on today's maps, only the word "Flat" has been added and the area is now known as Harrisburg Flat.

Pete Aguereberry and the writer were friends for nearly 20 years. I spent many happy days with him at the mine gathering notes for his biography. Many a night we sat at the dining table in the kitchen of his two-room cabin and talked all night. The sun would be coming up out of Death Valley when we went to bed.

I would sleep until noon in his three-room guest house which was clean and neat as a pin. After a brisk hike and breakfast (Pete did the cooking) we would go at it again. After four days of this, Pete would be all talked out. When we reached the point where he would cook and serve the meals in silence, I knew I had worn out my welcome and it was time to head for home at Trona. This was back in 1941, the year American Potash and Chemical Corporation's Trona plant was shut down for four and a half months by a labor strike. The plant is now owned and operated by Kerr-McGee Chemical Corporation. Inasmuch as I worked in the company-owned grocery store and people still had to eat, I worked every other week during the strike. On the off week I would drive back to Pete's place, taking some fresh meat and vegetables. The meat had to be cooked immediately as there was no refrigeration at the mine.

Pete would welcome me as if I were a long-lost brother, but after four days of talking, I would be on my way back to Trona. My story of Pete was run serially in the old *Trona Potash*, a weekly newspaper, which, at the time, was printed by the Hubbards in Randsburg.

The Basques are firm believers in the curative and healing power of hot mineral spring water. Late in 1945, Pete had been confined to the Trona Hospital. When he was released from the hospital, he cranked up his Model "A" Ford pickup truck and made a beeline for the hot springs at Tecopa, California. The springs were pretty crude in those days. They were not as widely known and used as the modern springs are today. In November of 1945, at the age of 72, Pete was found dead, floating face down in a spring. There was a bruise on the side of his face. The coroner surmised that he had gone in the spring alone in the night, stayed too long, became exhausted and in trying to climb out, had fallen, striking his head on the rock around the spring and drowned. Some of Pete's friends were skeptical of the verdict.

Perhaps to the coroner, Pete was just another old miner who had come to an untimely end in the badlands of the Amargosa Desert and who cared?

I, for one, thought perhaps there could have been foul play, inasmuch as his expensive trans-oceanic radio and his gold pocket watch were missing. He had won the watch at a track meet in the early days of Skidoo and it was engraved with his name. Also, most of the money he was supposed to be carrying was missing. I started an investigation but it did not go very far because the authorities were not concerned.

Pete is buried in the Mount Whitney Cemetery at Lone Pine. I was pallbearer at his funeral which was held in the Santa Rosa Catholic Church. The memorial mass was said by Father Fred Crowley, brother of the "great desert padre," Father John J. Crowley, who died in an automobile accident on Palm Sunday, March 17, 1940, near the intersection of Highways 14 and 178, about 15 miles west of Ridgecrest. There is a cross with rockwork along the side of the highway where he was killed.

Our story of Pete Aguereberry takes him practically from the cradle to the grave, just as he related it to me in his little cabin on Harrisburg Flat, high in the Panamint Mountains.

Pete left his footprints in the sands of time, for as long as the world lasts, there will always be an "Aguereberry Point" over-looking Death Valley.

●

CHAPTER I

JOURNEY *to the* LAND *of* PROMISE

Jean Pierre Aguereberry, whose name identifies one of the finest viewpoints overlooking Death Valley from the rim of the Panamint Mountains in Inyo County, California, was known to his friends as just plain "Pete." In earlier days he was called "French Pete." He was a Basque, born October 18, 1874, near the town of Mauleon on the French side of the Pyrenees.

When Pete was a boy, he lived on his father's farm which was ten hours walking distance from the Spanish border. He read in a French magazine about a great state in far away America, that was named California. The story stated that this was the land of golden opportunity and it painted a glowing picture of the fine vineyards, orchards, farms, ranches and gold mines that were found in California. Pete, after absorbing the story to the fullest extent, was filled with a burning desire to seek adventure and perhaps a fortune in this enchanted land that promised so much. He was to find high adventure and to turn down a fortune as you will read later on. He thumbed the pages of the magazine until they were worn as thin as his father's patience with his son's constant pleading to be allowed to go to this land of milk and honey, called California.

Papa Aguereberry didn't want to lose his Pierre, who was so young, only 15½ years of age and a half-orphan, as his mother had died when he was six years old. For a year he kept saying "no" to Pierre's pleas, but the boy's heart was set on going and it seemed that nothing was going to stop him. Finally, his irresistible entreaties (Pete called it bellyaching) wore his father down and he consented to Pete's going, with these words, "Get the hell out of here." Then with tears in his eyes he gave his son the money with which to make the trip. He probably would never have consented to Pete making the long journey into a foreign land at such a tender age but for the fact that an older brother, Arnaud, had immigrated to California seven years before and had settled in San Francisco. He knew that if Pete made the trip safely, Arnaud would take care of his younger brother.

Plans were made for Pete's journey. He was to accompany a party of fellow Basque emigrants who were leaving for America in a few weeks. His fare had been paid in advance to the travel agency. As all preparations for the journey had been completed, he was taking it easy, marking time until the day of departure arrived. Basking in the happy thoughts of the great adventure which lay before him and receiving congratulations from friends and neighbors on his coming journey, the days were indeed happy ones for Pete. But, just six days before he was to leave, disaster fell and Pete fell with it.

The month of November was chestnut harvesting time in the Pyrenees. A neighboring farmer had died and Pete was doing his bit for the family by thrashing the chestnuts and pruning the trees. Chestnut trees are very tall; the nuts are extremely hard to thrash and the trees are hard to prune. The thrasher climbed the tree carrying a long pole to knock the nuts from the tree. As this was extremely hazardous, it was usually performed by agile young fellows. Pete was considered one of the best. He had finished with the thrashing and was pruning when the accident happened. Braced between the fork of a limb, sawing away another limb, his mind was probably more on the coming journey than on what he was doing and he may have carelessly sawed off the wrong limb. However, the limb against which he was braced split off and down he plunged, crashing through the lower branches 45 feet to the ground below.

Poor Pete! Not only was his body broken but his heart was broken as well. With the thoughts of not being able to make the trip running through his mind, he was placed on a litter and carried to his home. The doctor was sent for—a local farmer who had never studied medicine or surgery in school. He found that Pete had a broken arm, three broken ribs, plus numerous cuts and bruises. The bruises didn't matter to Pete. After completing the examination, the doctor went to work on the patient. Two strong men were used for the anesthetic by holding Pete down. The

Basques are a hardy race of people and the country doctor did an efficient job. Pete was only confined to bed for three days. While he was bedridden the group of emigrants departed for America, leaving Pete behind. The days that followed were dark ones. Missing the trip hurt worse than the physical injuries and he was worried for fear of losing the money that had been paid in advance when he had contracted to leave on a specific date. However, these worries were alleviated somewhat when the travel agency granted a short extension.

Fifteen days from the time he fell from the tree, the time limit expired and Pete had to leave or lose the money. Starting the journey from the town of Mauleon, Papa Aguereberry, the relatives and most of the neighbors were there to see him off. It was a great day for Pete, and a sad one too, breaking the home ties, leaving his native land, probably never to see it again. Just a boy, only 16-years-old, still nursing his injuries with an arm in a sling, he faced the long journey ahead alone. When the train arrived, Pete struggled to get aboard amidst embraces, hand clasping, back slapping and shouted advice. A typical Basque send-off by those who had gathered at the station to bid him *au revoir*. Papa Aguereberry, with tears streaming down his cheeks, embraced for the last time, his Pierre, who was manfully fighting to hold back the tears. America had already claimed an older son, and now it was claiming another, young Pierre, who was going to join his brother in California. With one last embrace Pete pulled away from his father and scampered aboard the train, managing to obtain a seat in the compartment next to the window. As the train pulled out, he watched his father until he faded from view. He never saw him again.

Pete had been very brave, but now he was alone, and the tears came. He just couldn't hold them back any longer. Many times before he reached Bordeaux, wave after wave of homesickness engulfed him and he wished that he had never left home. He had ridden on a train but once before and that was when his father had taken him across the border into Spain to see a bullfight. Watching the telegraph poles flit past, with the surrounding landscape continually unfolding, and making acquaintance with other passengers in the compartment was indeed fascinating to Pete. However, there was one thing he couldn't understand, why the conductor locked the compartment door between stations. There were no lavatories in the coach but fortunately the towns in France were close together and the train stopped often. At each stop the conductor unlocked the door and the passengers were allowed to leave the train. When the conductor blew his whistle there was a mad scramble to get aboard.

When the train reached Bordeaux, Pete joined another party of emigrants who had been recruited by the same travel agency. They too, were going to America. Among them were a few Basques and it wasn't long until he made friends with them. By the time they reached Paris, his homesickness had been forgotten. They had a stop-over in Paris for two days while their passports were made up and Pete and his new found friends went on a tour of the city. They had planned to attend a theater in the evening, but the price of admission was five francs and that was entirely too steep for an emigrant's purse. Pete was more than compensated for having to miss the show when he spent his first night in a real hotel. The party reached Le Havre, where they embarked on the French ship, Chateau, on the following afternoon. So, on a cold November night in the year 1890, while Pete lay asleep in the bunk, the Chateau nosed out of the harbor. When he awoke in the morning, he was on the high seas bound for America.

The French emigrants were traveling second class. As the Chateau was a small ship, there was not much difference between second class and steerage, which was crowded with Italian emigrants. Food provided on the second class fare was so bad that the French would not eat it. As most of them had means to buy first class food, they gave the poor Italians the second class food, which was relished by them to the last crumb.

On the second day out, the ship was caught in a severe storm which reached its height at noon while the emigrants were eating. An enormous wave broke over the ship causing it to list so badly the food and dishes slid off the tables onto the floor. The salon and cabins were deluged with almost a foot of water, all of which added to the confusion and fright of the passengers. The ship's crew was busily engaged in pumping out the water, amidst a scene the likes of which Pete never wanted to see again. Women, some holding babies in their arms, were down on their knees in the water praying, some were hysterical, while others, both men and women, were violently seasick. After the storm subsided and things were serene again and the emigrants had recovered from the terrifying ordeal, Pete, who had never been seasick, was amusing himself at the expense of those who had, by imitating them in their agonies. He was rewarded for his grotesque gestures by a verbal barrage of "shut up" and had to dodge loose missles thrown at him.

Thirteen days out of Le Havre the ship docked in New York. Pete with his battered trunk, along with the rest of the emigrants, was herded into the custom station. Here Pete encountered his first problem on American soil, when called upon to declare his money for exchange. He was at a loss for a place of privacy away from the prying eyes of the curious emigrants, some of whom he didn't trust; a place where he could remove the gold coins carried in a money belt beneath his clothing without being seen. Sliding as far from view as possible, a convenient post offered partial concealment. Here he stripped off the belt, removed the gold and turned it over to the man in the cage, who in turn counted out a stack of American paper money and returned it to him. He pocketed the money, wondering if he had received fair exchange. It was all "Greek" to him. Not knowing the value of the strange money he was unable to count it and he couldn't speak English. Later, when trying to buy something, he would look around until he found what he wanted and then point it out to the sales person. Paying for the purchase offered the greatest problem. He never knew if he was being short-changed. Let us insert here, the Basque people we have known in our time were hard working, thrifty, honest and they were also very suspicious. They never seemed to completely trust anyone.

The emigrants were taken in tow by a French speaking guide who conducted them to a French hotel. As it was only a short distance from the custom house, they walked and enroute passed a park where Negro laborers were working. Pete had never seen Negroes before, so he stopped and gazed in awe at what he thought were wild men. The Negroes noticing the strangely dressed youth staring at them and presuming he was a "greenie" (old-country bumpkin), burst into laughter. Meanwhile, the party had gone on a ways before the guide missed Pete. Returning, he admonished him to keep up with the party as there were some pretty tough characters in this section of the city who would think nothing of slitting his throat for his money. After the warning he kept up with the group. In the environment of the hotel where everyone spoke French he felt more at ease, but when dinner was served, would wonders never cease? Here were more giant Negro wild men acting as waiters. At first he was afraid but when they spoke politely in French and when he noticed the ease and efficient manner with which they handled the great platters of food, he was more astonished than afraid.

After spending two days in New York, Pete began the long journey to California by train. It had taken 13 days to cross the Atlantic Ocean and coincidentally the same number of days to cross the continent. A stop-over between train changes in New Orleans allowed sufficient time for a visit to the French section of the city. His next recollection of train changes must have been in west Texas. All he could remember was a large depot completely isolated on a prairie. As night came on, the coyotes started howling. The emigrants thought they were wolves and they were a little frightened, knowing how ferocious the wolves were in the old country. It was in this depot that some of the Italian emigrants who had been fellow passengers on the ship were again encountered.

Pete never forgot the Italians, for in spite of their dire poverty and squalid condition they were a happy carefree lot. Each carried his personal belongings in a round bundle and some had small accordions which they would play at the slightest opportunity and, if circumstances permitted, the younger ones would break into a native dance. The merriment was in full swing in the waiting room of the station and Pete was part of the interested audience watching them perform. Eager-eyed, he never missed a thing and his curiosity was instantly aroused when he noticed the Italians occasionally stop and pick something from their body and put it in their mouth. Edging up closer to see, he was astonished to find that the Italians were infested with lice and were ridding themselves of the pesky ones by killing them with their teeth. Pete hastily retreated.

Rattling westward across the Texas plains, the train soon reached Indian country where Pete saw for the first time the American Redskin whom he had read so much about and with whom he had fought many an imaginary battle. At the stations along the way, half-naked Indian bucks surrounded the coaches offering pottery, bows, arrows and other trinkets for sale. No squaws were in evidence. Undoubtedly, they were still afraid to approach the "Iron Monster of the Big Noise."

Los Angeles stood out in his mind as the town of a thousand shanties, where the train's arrival at the depot caused a team of horses to run away up Main Street, scattering pedestrians right and left. Oakland was reached during the night. Crossing the bay by ferryboat under a dense blanket of fog, the constant din of a foghorn heralded the arrival of Jean Pierre Aguereberry to the city of San Francisco in the year 1890.

CHAPTER II

COURTING DISASTER

At last Pete reached the city of his dreams. The long journey from his home in the French Pyrenees, which had required a month's time was now ended; the journey which he had begun while still nursing the injuries received by falling from the chestnut tree. The smashed ribs had healed long ago and the broken arm was as good as new, but when he arrived in San Francisco Pete was ill.

He had always been a husky lad. Never sick a day in his life—unless one counted the time he drank too much of his father's sour wine. This happened when he was 12 years old. He had never drunk any wine before. His father had never forbidden him to drink, neither had he given him permission and Pete had never asked. He had watched his older brothers go into the wine cellar and sip wine through a straw from a barrel. He thought he would try it. The day was warm and the wine was cool, so he sipped and sipped. To him, it was like drinking water. He did not know the wine would make him sick, but he soon found out. It hit him when he was driving the cows to pasture and he had to lie down in the shade of a tree. When he did not return on schedule his folks began to worry and they called the neighbors who were working in nearby fields to help look for him. When found, he was gently carried home and put to bed. However, this was not the end of his trouble. The straying cows had ruined a neighbor's garden and he had left the bung out of the wine barrel and hundreds of flies had fallen into the wine. The next morning his father flailed the living daylights out of him and he was sick all over again.

At last brother Arnaud came to the station for him and as they had not seen each other for seven years, it was a joyous occasion. He tried to hide the illness from his brother, but the cough he couldn't hold back gave him away. Arnaud realizing the boy was sick, hustled him off to his hotel room and put him to bed. He figured that after a few days rest Pete would be all right but the cough continued to grow worse. Arnaud became alarmed thinking perhaps the boy had tuberculosis and that he had better call a doctor. However, when Pete had a severe coughing spell, Arnaud discovered he was wormy and only needed some medicine to kill the worms. A French woman who lived in the hotel obliged by brewing the right herbs. In three days the worms were gone and Pete was well.

Pete spent the next few days getting acquainted with San Francisco. It was a gay city and a rough one in the days before the great earthquake and fire. The street lights were gas; street cars were horse drawn and underground Chinatown was a place to be avoided unless accompanied by a guide. Gas lights were something new in Pete's life, something he did not understand. One night when they were retiring, Arnaud caught Pete in the act of blowing out the gas light. After the lecture he received from Arnaud, Pete was educated about the dangers of gas. After two weeks of sightseeing he began to look for a job. It wasn't easy due to his youth and inability to speak English, which handicapped him greatly. Most French Basques arriving in this country in those days followed the bakery or laundry trade. Many of them became sheepherders since they didn't have to speak English to herd sheep. Pete knew nothing about these trades. All he knew was farming and farming could not be done in the city.

Finally, through his brother Arnaud, he landed his first job in America. He couldn't believe his good fortune, this was not work, it was play. Arnaud was employed in a bakery and for recreation he played handball, a game originated and introduced to America by the Basques. Pete, as an athlete, excelled in two sports, running and handball, so Arnaud took him down to Irish MacDonald's handball court. He figured on giving his younger brother a lesson on how the game was played. Arnaud underestimated his brother's ability to play the game and took a shellacking. Irish MacDonald, ever on the alert for good players, was watching them play. When the game ended, he hired Pete on the spot. He was to play for his expenses. It wasn't much, but it was a job and he didn't have to speak English to play handball.

Due to his youth and hard playing, he immediately became a favorite with the fans. Whenever he stepped onto the court to play, the rousing ovation from the gallery was sweet music to his ears and he loved it. This and the satisfaction of knowing that he was holding his own against the tough Irish players buoyed him to great heights. The game as played in this country had been modified somewhat, a smaller and harder ball was used. Pete, accustomed to playing the softer ball off the palm of his hand, was playing the harder ball the same way when it should have been played from the fingers. Consequently, he developed a sore hand that became so painful that at the end of two weeks he was forced to quit the game.

It was a tough blow, down-hearted and discouraged he wanted to leave San Francisco and shortly the opportunity presented itself. Most Basques of the day were ardent handball fans. The wealthy sheep owners came from their ranches in the San Joaquin Valley to attend the games in San Francisco. Pete had met a few of them and when he had to quit the game, one of them offered him a job herding sheep. The pay was to be $25.00 a month and grub. Pete knew nothing about sheepherding and he told the man so. However, he was quickly assured that it was an easy job and that anyone could become a sheepherder, especially a Basque. The Basque sheep owners were keen on hiring members of their own race because they were dependable, hardworking and loyal. Pete accepted the job. Bidding his brother and San Francisco goodbye, he accompanied his employer to the town of Huron, west of Hanford in the San Joaquin Valley. Here he began his career as a sheepherder.

As the shearing season was near at hand, he was started out with a band of 2,600 sheep with instructions to range them in the immediate vicinity until shearing time. For a beginner he got along quite well, with the exception of having a difficult time becoming accustomed to sleeping on the ground and learning to cook. At first his culinary efforts were pretty crude. He soon learned that when cooking rice one used very little rice and a lot of water. On his first attempt he used very little water and a lot of rice. When the rice started boiling over, it filled all the utensils he had, even the dishpan. He fed the chipmunks a lot of cooked rice.

For an amateur, he was doing well, he had even begun to think that sheepherding was a fine job. As it was springtime, the range afforded ample feed for the sheep and they were well-behaved. Only old Pacho, the name Pete had given his burro, was troublesome. Pacho had been with sheep so long that he was lonesome without them. When they moved, he moved with them regardless of whether Pete had the camping equipment packed on his back or not. Many a time he would break away while Pete was in the midst of packing and scatter the camping equipment right and left. These occurrences afforded him the opportunity to exercise his vocabulary of cuss words.

Pete had worked at sheepherding a little over a month when the shearing season started. Driving his band into the big corrals at Huron where the shearing sheds were located and seeing that they were safely corraled, he was confident that he had it made as a sheepherder. As he had made the first month with little trouble, he was beginning to believe the boss was right about the job being easy—ah! poor Pete, if he had only known how ornery sheep can be at times and the trouble they were to cause him in the future, he would have lost the cocksureness in a hurry.

Huron was a great shearing center in the '90's, more than 200 shearers were employed at the height of the season. Enormous corrals held more sheep than Pete imagined there were in the world. Everyone was busy at shearing time and Pete was soon engulfed in the maelstrom of toil, sweat, dust and the noise of bleating sheep. The shearers rolled up great piles of wool, and then permitted their near-naked victims to scamper wildly away following the last snip of the shears. There, also, was an old mule plodding around and around the well, motivating power for the pump that lifted water for the sheep. All this was a new and interesting sight for Pete.

After a month of loneliness on the range, alone with the sheep, Pete was thoroughly enjoying the companionship of the Basques. In the evenings sitting around the campfires they would tell stories, sing and talk about their homes in the far away Pyrenees. Infrequently, the conversation would drift to sports, and it was only natural that some of the younger ones would mildly boast of their prowess in some given sport. Once Pete modestly mentioned that he had won a few races back in the old country. No one seemed to put much stock in this statement until a day or two later when he unintentionally backed up the statement by winning an odd race against a sheep that had escaped from a corral. Pete ran the sheep down, catching it in the presence of a couple of sheep owners.

There was a sheep shearer in camp who had the reputation of being the fastest runner in the sheep country. The two owners began to talk up a race between Pete and the shearer. In due time the match was made. The race was to take place on the following Sunday afternoon, and during the ensuing time, the betting rivalry ran high. The 200 sheep shearers, to the last man, were backing their runner. The owners and herders were just as spirited in their backing of Pete. Sunday afternoon everyone knocked off from work to see the race and to root for his particular favorite. The race was to be 500 yards. After the distance was measured off and all preparations completed, the contestants toed the mark awaiting the crack of the starter's gun. The shearer was overly anxious and jumped the gun. Pete did not start. He thought his opponent, having made a false start, would stop and return for a new start, but he kept on going. Pete's backers, with visions of their bets flying away on the winged feet of the shearer, started yelling, "Run, Pete, run!" Pete started, and how he started, as though he was shot out of a gun, but could he overtake the speeding shearer who, by his unfair start, now had a big lead? "Come on Pete," was shouted from all sides and Pete came on. Gaining rapidly he caught his opponent in the last five yards, and with a superhuman effort threw himself against the tape, a step ahead of the shearer. Pete was now the fair-haired boy among the sheepmen, the toast of the camp, so to speak. Most anything he desired was his for the asking, except one thing. He could not get any more matched races, not even with a sheep.

The first day after leaving Huron with his flock of sheep, Pete made camp. Sometime during the night a cold rain set in. Having just been relieved of their winter overcoats, the poor sheep had to do something to keep warm so they started traveling. When Pete awoke, they were gone. Jumping out of his blankets he became panicky, fearing that if he lost the sheep, he would also lose his job.

Scouting around in the darkness, he heard the faint tinkle of the leader's bell in the distance. Losing his head completely, he ran through the darkness toward the sound of the bell. In his headlong rush he plunged into a dry creek bed, falling 15 feet to the boulders below. When he regained consciousness, he was lying on his back with the rain beating on his face. Terrible pain wracked his body and he was unable to move. The rain continued and water started running in the dry creek bed, gradually rising inch by inch. Pete, lying there in agony in the darkness, felt he was beyond human aid. Stark fear overwhelmed him as the water rose higher and higher. If it continued, it would only be a matter of time until he would drown like a rat in a hole. Thoughts of dying so young kept running through his mind, as he prayed feverishly for the all merciful God to save him. His prayers were answered as the rain stopped and the water receded.

When daylight came he found that he had a broken ankle. He could not walk or bear the pain of trying to crawl. The only way he could travel was by walking on his knees, while reaching behind to hold the injured ankle off the ground by grasping the cuff of his pant leg. Following the line of least resistance, slowly and painfully he made his way down the creek bed, hoping to find a road crossing the creek where, by chance, someone passing along would find him before it was too late. It was noon before he came to a road and none too soon, as he had about reached the limit of his endurance. He had covered about a mile and a half. His pants were worn through and his knees were bloody and raw. Collapsing along the side of the road, he lay there helpless. Luck was with him, for a few minutes later, a sheep owner came along in a wagon and found him. Pete was never so glad to see anyone in his life as he was to see this man. After giving Pete water and hearing his story, the sheep owner asked, "Where are the sheep?" Pete told him that he did not know where they were and furthermore, he did not care.

Loading Pete on the wagon, the sheep owner told him to drive back to camp while he went hunting for the sheep, for, after all, the sheep were worth more than a herder. Pete was hardly able to sit on the wagon seat, much less drive, but he had no choice. Several times he almost fell from the wagon. Each time he managed to grab hold of the seat to prevent the fall. As he lurched about he frightened the mules, causing them to run away, nearly upsetting the wagon. A man in camp saw the runaway and rode out to catch the team. Driving into camp, Pete was lifted from the wagon and laid on the ground. Unlacing the boot they tried to pull it off, but Pete yelled bloody murder. The ankle was so swollen the boot had to be cut off. After administering what first aid they could, Pete was loaded back on the wagon, where he was hauled into Huron and put on the train for Fresno.

On his arrival he was taken to a hotel run by a Basque. The sheep owners used the hotel as a convalescent home for injured sheepherders. Sickness among the herders was something unheard of in those days. Most of them were young and their life in the wide open spaces, coupled with the plain and wholesome food they ate, made them about the healthiest people known. Accidents, however were not uncommon. Pete did not recall if there was a hospital in Fresno at the time. Probably not, as this was 1891. When Pete reached the hotel, he was carried upstairs and put to bed. A doctor was called and when he arrived to examine the broken ankle he found it was very serious due to the great length of time which had elapsed since the injury occurred. The ankle and leg were badly swollen.

Today it is hard for us to visualize the problems confronted by medical men and the suffering their patients endured nearly a century ago. Pete's case was an example where the doctor set the broken bone in a badly swollen ankle without the aid of X-ray or an anesthetic. It's true that anesthetics had been discovered and put into use long before this happened. Why one was not administered to Pete to relieve his suffering is not known. Perhaps none was available in Fresno at the time or else the doctor did not deem it advisable to use an anesthetic in setting broken bones, or maybe they just didn't waste it on sheepherders.

The doctor, after setting the bone, used tin splints with eyeholes similar to those in a boot, in lieu of a cast. The splints were laced tightly around the ankle. Before leaving, the doctor warned Pete that the tightness of the splints would hurt considerably, but, no matter how much it pained him, he was not to relieve the pressure by loosening the laces. It did hurt immensely. Pete tolerated it as long as he could and then he would loosen the laces. He always managed to have them laced tightly before the doctor called, however.

After a few days, with the aid of crutches, he was able to be up and around. At first he was pretty awkward on the crutches, especially when descending the stairs. Pete never forgot the grand entrance he made into the dining room one night. Very carefully, he made his way down to the next to the last step on the stairs. There, he lost his balance and fell forward. The crutches, acting as a catapult, hurled him head first through the swinging doors and he slid into the dining room on his stomach. Momentarily stunned, the astonished diners quickly helped him up. In addition to the pain from the bump on his head, the ankle hurt much worse. Fortunately, it was not rebroken. Having completely lost his appetite, he was carried back upstairs and put to bed. Next day, feeling no ill effects from the spill, he was back on the crutches fully determined to master them. Before long he became so proficient that he was entertaining the guests with acrobatic stunts around the lobby with two other sheepherders who were also on crutches. Luckily he didn't break the ankle again, or his neck, with his madcap antics.

CHAPTER III

THE LONELY TRAIL

After convalesing for six weeks Pete was able to return to work. Rejoining his band of sheep, his instructions were to drive them northward to a point near Stockton in the Sacramento Valley, where they were to be ranged for the summer in the tules. Two other bands of sheep were being driven to the same area so he had company on the drive. Each sheepherder had to keep his herd away from the other to prevent mixing. Even so, they made good time with the sheep traveling as much as 26 miles on good days.

Everything went well until they were approaching Modesto. They encountered extremely hot weather and a long stretch of country that was waterless. For two days the traveling sheep were without water. They were so thirsty that when they neared the Tuolumne River and smelled the water, they stampeded for the river. The bank of the river at that point was 30 to 40 feet high. The poor thirst-crazed sheep plunged over the steep bank into the water. Out of the 8,000 being driven by the three herders, 1,500 of them were killed by the fall or were drowned.

What a mess! The herders and their dogs worked like mad to prevent the catastrophe but to no avail. After it was all over, they wearily rounded up the remaining 6,500, driving them into corrals near Modesto where they began the tiresome task of separating the sheep by their brands. Who said that sheepherding was an easy job? Baa! Baa!

There was a law at the time requiring that all dead sheep had to be burned or buried. Pete's boss was arrested and fined for not complying with the law. Pete wondered how one was to burn or bury 1,500 dead sheep when they were all in the river?

Pete spent the first summer as a sheepherder in the tules near

Modesto. Fall found him moving the sheep leisurely southward down the great San Joaquin Valley. There was good grazing land around Los Banos, Huron, the foothills near Coalinga and in the Kettleman Hills. Pete, grazing his sheep over these rolling hills, never dreamed that deep in the ground beneath his feet were vast cavities full of black liquid gold, that in later years, when tapped by drillers' bits, would become one of California's richest oil fields.

The Basques had acquired a lot of this country for grazing and ranching. They had gained title to the land in a subtle manner that bordered slightly on what would be known today as a racket. The method used was to help their countrymen come to this country and have them squat on the land. When the required seven years had elapsed, they would help them become American citizens, thereby entitled to homestead the land. Then, the sheep men would buy the land for little or nothing, paying the homesteader a couple of hundred dollars at the most.

Many years ago a news item appeared in the *San Francisco Chronicle* that coincides with the story at this point, and we quote: "Edouard Estrem, last known address, the Pyrenees, France, needed 'Superman' and a fast trip to Oakland. He did not get it and today, Edouard is just an executor. Edouard's uncle, Jean Estrem, once was a Fresno sheep owner who after buying a chunk of grazing land, went back to Belgium to die. The grazing land turned out to be the center of the Kettleman Hills oil field. In a will written in Oakland and admitted to probate there, his nephew was named executor. The court wrote to Edouard but mail and transportation service is irregular in France. Not knowing whether Edouard was Oakland-bound, the court under law had to turn the estate over to the Public Administrator. Its value has been estimated at $1 million."

Pete was a sheepherder for three long years during which time he made three great loops around the High Sierra Nevada Mountains. There was a big shearing camp at Poso near Bakersfield. After the sheep had been sheared there in the springtime, they would be grazed south through the Tehachapi Mountains. Emerging from the mountains above Mojave they would swing east skirting through what was later known as Searles Station and on into Indian Wells Valley. Continuing on north through Owens Valley in Inyo County and further north through Mono County into Alpine County, from there they would swing northwest sometimes going as far north as Sacramento, before returning to the San Joaquin Valley.

In dry years the route was altered a little. Upon emerging from the Tehachapi Mountains they swung northeast and used Jawbone Canyon as an access to the Piute Mountains. Coming out of the Piutes through Kelso Valley to Weldon in the Kern River Valley, they would follow the South Fork of the Kern River into the high country, through the Honeybee District into the beautiful Monache Meadows. Here they went out of the mountains down Oak Creek Canyon coming out at Olancha in Owens Valley.

On these long treks with the sheep Pete had his share of thrilling adventure and hardship, but he took them in stride for it was all part of the game. There were times when his blankets were soaked by rain. He would tie one end of the blanket to whatever was handy to wring out the water. There were times when he slept in wet blankets in the mud. There were times when he was pelted by hail and there were times when he packed a full grown sick sheep on his back for miles into camp and doctored it back to health. In his three years as a herder he only slept in a tent two weeks. Many times he would go for weeks without seeing a soul. Supplies were hauled in by wagon and left at his camp. If Pete happened to be out with the sheep, he would miss seeing the driver. The driver seldom made any attempt to locate Pete, or wait in camp until he returned, simply taking for granted that Pete was all right.

Sheepherding had its brighter moments, and when they came Pete took full advantage of them. With the coming of spring when the good earth became alive with life, the birds, the small animals, even the insects were his friends and companions. The flowers and everything that grew offered solace to him in his solitude. At night millions of stars were his guardians. Pete's shepherd dog, his constant companion, was an exceptionally intelligent animal and Pete was greatly attached to him. The bond between them seemed almost human. When Pete collected wood or brush for his cooking fire the dog worked alongside his master, gathering the material for the fire in his mouth. If Pete left his hat in camp and wanted it, all he had to do was put his hand on his head and say, "Get it," and the dog never failed to do so. To a humble sheepherder, like Pete, $100 was a lot of money in those days. He was offered that amount for his dog and he declined the offer. He would not have sold the dog for any amount of money.

(When the author was a small boy in 1911 and 1912, living in the oil fields a few miles northwest of Coalinga in the foothills, he remembers the numerous bands of sheep that grazed by his home and the occasions when a friendly sheepherder would give him a motherless lamb for a pet. This was 18 years after Pete herded his sheep through that area.)

When sheep are on the move traveling from range to range as the seasons progress, two herders are usually required to drive a band of 2,600 sheep. In the mountains, when a base camp had been set up for the summer, a herder could handle as many as 3,500 alone. Pete enjoyed the mountains, for here the job of herding sheep was at its best. He enjoyed the cool nights and pleasant days as he leisurely followed the sheep. Owing to the abundance of lush grass that grew in the mountain meadows, it was unnecessary for the sheep to forage any great distance from camp.

With time on his hands, Pete had a chance to learn many tricks of the trade. One that he chose to tell about stood out above the rest and could be appropriately entitled, "Fooling the Ewe." This was how it was done. If a ewe's lamb died and another ewe had twins, the dead lamb would be skinned and the skin tied on one of the twins, which would then be placed with the ewe who had lost her lamb. Ewes will not nurse another's lamb. They recognize their offspring through sense of smell. Thus, when the strange lamb was placed with the ewe, she would sniff the skin and thinking it was her own, permit it to nurse contentedly. One might wonder why this was done. The explanation is that when a ewe has twins, one of them never gets enough milk and usually dies. By fooling the ewe, Pete saved many lambs.

Pete also enjoyed the mountains for another reason, namely for the abundance of small game and fish that kept his larder supplied with fresh meat. The mountain streams were teeming with trout and when he wanted a mess, he never bothered catching them with a hook and line. That was far too slow. What he did was to take a shovel and throw a dam across a small stream diverting the water over the bank, causing it to spread out on higher ground, thus leaving the helpless trout high and dry. When enough fish were trapped, he broke the dam. If there were a surplus they were smoked and dried for future use. The mountains also afforded him the opportunity of matching his wit against the bear and mountain lions that preyed on the sheep. His dog would always give the alarm when a varmint was stalking the sheep. Pete would grab his trusty firearm, which was an old single-barrel shotgun loaded with buckshot, and go on the run. Usually he would be in time to save the sheep. Between the dog's barking and Pete's yelling the varmint would be scared away most of the time, but if not, Pete would bang away. Buckshot is deadly at close range and Pete became pretty good as a marksman. More than once he skinned out a mountain lion.

Pete also had to match wits with the cattlemen who bitterly resented the sheep's invasion of the grazing land in the mountains or any other grazing land for that matter. The cowpunchers were plenty tough in those days, as were sheepherders. The two were continuously at dagger's point. Many were the times that some luckless sheepherder was the recipient of a severe beating at the hands of the cowpunchers. However, Pete was lucky and escaped being physically abused, though he was on the receiving end of much verbal abuse, especially if the sheep had broken through a ranger's fence. Their verbal abuse didn't hurt Pete because he did not understand English except for a few cuss words he picked up around the sheep camps. You can bet the cattlemen threw plenty at him. When they would try to question him all he could say was, "No savvy," a phrase used by the Mexicans when they didn't wish to understand English. This only aroused the cattlemen's anger more and it's a wonder he ever escaped the beatings. When the cowpunchers tired of eating their own beef and wanted mutton for a change, they obtained it by setting wire snares in the thickets in the path of the sheep. Pete soon caught onto this and he kept the sheep away from the thickets as much as possible.

Pete spoke five languages, two of the Basque, French, Italian and Spanish. He was trying to learn English, but sheepherding offered little opportunity, since he spent little time in sheep camps with other herders who spoke English. He tried to learn by picking up an object, say for example a knife or fork, and asking the English name. Instead of teaching him the correct name he would be given an obscene one by the herders. His education continued in this manner until he tried to converse with a ranch woman in English. She was highly insulted and called her husband who chased Pete off the ranch. Poor Pete did not know why he was treated in this manner, but later on when he discovered why, he was so ashamed that it was three years before he found the courage to attempt to talk to an American woman.

It has previously been said in the story that Pete circled the Sierra Nevada Mountains of California three times. These circuits were made between 1892 and 1894. The final tour was the year of the great drought in 1894 when all the sheep men went broke. It was also the year that Pete got his first smell of a gold rush while grazing his sheep near the Rand District. Gold strikes were made in Golar Canyon and at Summit Diggins. Gold, the magic word, had everyone in the vicinity excited except the lowly sheepherders who were experiencing excitement from another cause. The sheep were dying likes flies for lack of grass and water. The year 1894 was the driest in the annals of eastern California. What little grass there was dried up and died in early spring. The water holes were dry and most of the mountain streams were dry. The sheep men lost 200,000 head of sheep that year and sheep carcasses were scattered from Tehachapi to Bridgeport.

It was the custom in those days for the sheepherders to allow their bosses to keep their wages. Pete's wages were $25.00 a month with grub and clothing. The boss acted as their banker and most of the herders never drew any of their pay until they quit. In Pete's case he had three years' pay in the boss's keeping. With the sheep starving to death and the sheep men going broke, Pete showed his loyalty to a fellow Basque, his boss, by lending him his back pay, trying to help tide him over. Pete's meager effort to help went for naught and they all went broke together. All the money Pete ever received for his three years' work as a sheepherder was a $10.00 bill the boss gave him to get home.

CHAPTER IV

A NEW BEGINNING

Pete went home to his brother Arnaud, who was now living in Madera. Arnaud, along with a partner, had leased and was operating a fruit and barley ranch. Pete was now 20 years old. The three years spent in the open with the sheep had developed him into a husky, healthy lad, well suited for the hard ranch work. He worked on his brother's ranch until his 21st birthday and upon reaching manhood, struck out on his own.

With an eye to becoming a stage driver he went to work for the Washburn Stage Line, whose advertisement claimed their line to be the finest in all America. If it was not the finest in the country, as far as horses, equipment and service were concerned, there was no question about its being the most scenic. The line operated between the town of Raymond on the Southern Pacific Railroad and Yosemite Park. One of the highlights along its route was where the stagecoach passed through a giant redwood tree. There are probably few households in our country that have not at sometime or another received a picture post card of this huge tree from a tourist in the Golden Bear State. It was Pete's one ambition to some day drive a stagecoach through the big redwood tree. His inconspicuous start with the stage company left him with a long uphill pull if he were to attain his goal.

He started at the bottom of bottoms, so to speak. The stage company owned and operated a large ranch near Madera, where they raised their own horses, cows and foodstuff. The cows furnished fresh milk for the eating houses along the stage route. Pete went to work with the haying crew. The work was only temporary, ending when the haying was done. Pete had worked so hard and faithfully, that when the job was done, all the crew was laid off except him. He was now assured of a steady job on the ranch, starting out doing the usual ranch chores—one of which was to irrigate the alfalfa.

One winter day, Pete, with his dog, was out irrigating, when the dog kept barking at something in the alfalfa. He went over to see what the dog had found. He had never seen a skunk before and he thought that it was a pretty cat with a striped back. He also thought it strange that the dog kept at a respectful distance from the animal when he had seen the dog do battle with the big house cats at the barn. Thinking that it would be nice to catch the animal, take it up to the ranch house and show it to the folks and perhaps feed it some milk, he pulled off his coat and used it to make the catch. Pete soon realized he had made a mistake for he had never smelled such a bad odor in his life. Quickly, he turned the animal loose, but not before his only coat was ruined. Eventually, he had to burn the coat, when he found that after repeated washings the odor still remained.

Before going to the ranch house for dinner, Pete stripped and scrubbed and scrubbed and put on clean clothes. When he entered the dining room, the woman who was serving the meal called to her husband. "Charlie, oh Charlie, there's a skunk in the house." Charlie came and searched the house high and low, but he never found the skunk. Pete could understand English quite well now and he could speak it a little, but in this ticklish situation he felt he was not versed enough to explain to them that he was the skunk for whom they were searching. Excusing himself, he left the house and hurried over to a neighboring ranch where a Frenchman lived who spoke English. Telling him the story, he got him to come over and explain to Charlie and his wife what had happened. They took it as a joke and had a big laugh.

After the skunk escapade, Pete was promoted to a job in the dairy, which was a most unusual dairy when compared with the dairies of today that deliver milk in containers. Due to the lack of refrigeration and to ensure the patrons of their eating houses along the stage route fresh milk, the stage company shipped the milk in the original container. They shipped the cows. It was Pete's job to take care of the dairy herd, some 40 cows, to wean the calves early and keep the eating houses supplied with fresh cows.

Pete worked for the stage line for a year and a half. He never realized his ambition to drive a stagecoach through the big redwood; however, he did get to drive a fast freight wagon through the tree. This came about when 1,500 members of the Christian Endeavor Society of San Francisco held a convention in Yosemite. The sudden influx of passengers so overtaxed the stage line's facilities and drivers, that Pete was drafted to drive the fast freight wagon which hauled their baggage in and out of the park.

When Pete left the employ of the Washburn Stage Line, the haying season was at hand. He joined a migrant haying crew who were following the season. The ranchers fed the haying crews, but did not furnish them with sleeping quarters. The hayers carried bedrolls and slept on the ground in the fields. They worked from daylight until dark seven days a week. One day the crew finished a field at noon and moved on to a new field a short distance away. As they walked along with their bedrolls slung on their backs, Pete kept hearing a buzzing sound that seemed to come from his bedroll. At first he paid little attention to the sound but as it continued at short intervals, his curiosity was aroused and he asked a companion to listen to the sound. The companion listened for a moment and then said, "Pete, I believe you're packing a rattlesnake in your bedroll."

Pete wasted no time in unslinging the bedroll. Dropping it to the ground, untying the cords and spreading it out, he carefully removed the blankets one by one as the buzzing grew louder and louder. When he removed the last blanket, there was the angry rattler. As he killed the snake, he thanked his lucky star that they had moved from the last field at noon and not spent the night there. Had they spent the night he would have crawled into the blankets with the snake. He shuddered at the thought of what the consequence might have been.

As far back as Pete could remember, he had always had a horror of snakes, for good reason. His mother had died from the poisonous bite of a viper. He was only six years old at the time, but he remembered every detail of the heartbreaking tragedy as clearly as though it had happened yesterday. There was a sadness in his voice and a glistening of tears in the dim eyes as he told of the death of his mother.

Each Basque farmhouse in the Pyrenees Mountains had an outdoor oven in which the family bread was baked. One day his mother was making the necessary preparations for baking on the following day. She was out at dusk gathering wood for a fire. When she returned to the house, she complained of having pricked her hand on a sharp object and that it was very painful. She would raise the hand to her mouth and suck the wound to relieve the pain. No one paid particular attention to her at the time, but when she became violently ill and the arm began swelling, they realized she had been bitten by a poisonous snake. Hurriedly they sent for the doctor, but when he arrived, it was too late. Pete's mother had passed on. The next morning the viper was found where she had been gathering the wood.

CHAPTER V

LOVE GOES AGLIMMERING

It was while working as a hayer that Pete became acquainted with some miners who worked at the Dalton Mine near Madera. He was fascinated by the swashbuckling miners who were always bragging about only working nine hours a day and the good wages they made, while he was working in the hayfields from daylight to dark for a wage which was meager indeed when compared with the miner's pay. To get a job at the mine and make those big wages became an obsession with him. One day when the miners stopped at the ranch for water and a bit of gossip, Pete made his desire known. Sure, they would speak to the boss. And it came to pass, he was hired at the mine as a mucker. Working underground was a new adventure for him, and he soon learned that even though the pay was good, a fellow earned every cent of it, for the work was hard as well as dangerous. He also learned that the miners were a rough, hard-drinking lot, some of whom delighted in making life miserable for a greenhorn like himself.

One fellow in particular, a big Italian, was a past master at the art of bullying and he gave Pete his undivided attention. It was annoying enough when he would hide Pete's hat and other pieces of wearing apparel, even his tools; but the times when he would draw Pete into a sparring match and cuff him around were the most difficult and trying. Pete took it as long as he could and one day he cuffed back a little too strongly, making the Italian angry. Whereupon, he unleashed a terrific kidney punch, knocking Pete colder than a dead mackerel. A big blacksmith at the mine decided the Italian had carried his bullying far enough; going to Pete's defense, he ran the Italian out of camp.

By this time, Pete had his fill of mining and the rough treatment received at the hands of the tough miners, so he quit and returned to Madera where he obtained a job with the Italian Swiss Colony Winery. Pete worked at the winery for nearly a year. It was here he made the acquaintance of a fellow Basque who owned the French Liquor Store in Madera. When the wine merchant came to the winery for his weekly supply of wine, he and Pete would banter back and forth in their native tongue. In the course of time they became fast friends and Pete was not surprised when he was offered a job in the liquor store. Reluctantly, he quit the winery and went to work for his new found friend.

Pete found the job pleasant and he enjoyed the work, as the store was patronized mostly by the French and Spanish Basque inhabitants of the town. Out in back of the store there was a typical old country outdoor wine garden, where the patrons would sit in the cool of the evening and sip the good California wine, served them by Pete for 15 cents a quart. The men played cards for drinks, and spun yarns of the old country. At times there were native songs and dances enjoyed by both sexes. It was here that Pete met Rosa.

Rosa was a dark-eyed senorita and a beauty. Being a friend of the boss's wife she came often to visit. From the first, Pete was fond of her and when he began making eyes at her, he was rewarded by shy blushing glances, which told him the feeling was mutual. It wasn't long until they were sweethearts. Everything seemed rosy to Pete, for he was in love. They both liked to dance, which they did at every opportunity. Rosa was a popular girl and the other young men of the town were always vying with Pete for her dances. Occasionally on Sunday, Pete would hire a horse and buggy and take Rosa for a ride in the country. It was on such an occasion when Pete's love castle came tumbling down. His dreams were shattered and Rosa was no longer his sweetheart. It came about when Pete made a date during the week to take his Rosa for a ride the following Sunday. To be sure of obtaining a horse and buggy before they were all hired out, he went down to the livery stable on Saturday and made arrangements for the rig.

Early Sunday morning when he called for Rosa, she could not go. She was all apologies and awfully sorry, her excuse was that out-of-town relatives were coming to visit for the day and she would have to stay home and help her mother with the cooking. Sadly disappointed, Pete returned the rig to the livery stable and prepared to pass the day as best he could. He owned a bicycle and it was such a fine day he went for an afternoon spin in the country. Pedaling along down lover's lane he overtook a buggy. Rapidly passing, he threw up his arm in greeting. Something about the occupants of the buggy seemed familiar, so he slowed down to take a better look. Then he wished he hadn't, for there in the buggy was his Rosa with another man. Pain and anger raged within him and he pumped the pedals off the bicycle for the next few miles. Long before his anger cooled, he had lost faith in women. Consequently, he was a free man all of his life as he never married.

In the late 1890's the old west still lived in the San Joaquin Valley. Usually, differences of opinion were settled the American way, with fists flying, but infrequently the flashing blade of a knife found its mark in the body of a victim and roaring guns spelled murder. One night in a Los Banos saloon, Pete saved a friend, the saloon-keeper, from being stabbed in the back, only to see him murdered an hour later by a roaring gun in the hand of the same assailant. The saloon-keeper, a Basque, was playing in a poker game. Pete was sitting at the end of the bar near the game watching the play. One of the players, who was losing consistently, lost his temper and accused the saloon-keeper of cheating. Hot words were exchanged and the two men almost came to blows. The argument ended when the trouble-maker was ordered from the game. He left the saloon in a rage. A short time later he was back with his temper apparently under control. As he casually sauntered up behind the saloon-keeper, the players, intent upon the game did not notice him. Pete, who had seen him enter the saloon, could tell by his actions that he was up to no good, and he kept an eye on him. Well that he did, for when the man was directly behind the saloon-keeper, he whipped a knife from his belt. Pete lunged from the bar stool in time to grab the man's arm, preventing his friend, the saloon-keeper, from being stabbed in the back.

After a brief struggle, the man was disarmed and thrown bodily out of the saloon, with orders to stay out. He was soon back with a gun and he shot the saloon-keeper before anyone could make a move. With the smoking gun in his hand, he wheeled and dashed out of the saloon, mounted his horse and galloped away.

The drumming hoof beats of the running horse on the wooden bridge at the edge of the little town echoed the murderer's escape from the infuriated townsmen. Months later the murderer was apprehended by the law and was brought to justice.

Seven years after his arrival in the United States, Pete received his naturalization papers and became an American citizen. The year was 1897 and he was working in the orchards around Fresno as a pruner. This was a proud day for the gentle Basque.

In 1898, the year of the Spanish-American War, he returned to San Francisco and secured a job as a milk wagon driver. Fresh milk was delivered in cans, each customer furnishing his own container. Leaving San Francisco in the winter of 1899, Pete went to Elko, Nevada, where he was employed as a ranch hand on the Spanish Ranch. The Spanish Ranch laid claim to being the largest and oldest in the state of Nevada. Its enormous range extended for a distance of 75 miles. Starting the ranch shortly after the California gold rush, a Spaniard by the name of Palo Alto had wrested a fortune from the seemingly arid country by raising cattle, horses and sheep.

Palo Alto had two sons, Bernard and Pedro, a wealthy pair of dashing caballeros, who cut quite a swath through the sporting life of San Francisco before the turn of the century. With the passing of their father, the sons became sole heirs to the ranch. Quitting San Francisco, they returned to Nevada, accompanied by French Basque brides, to take over the reins of the ranch. Pete had made the acquaintance of the brothers at the handball courts where he played at his first job in San Francisco. When he tired of city life, he followed the Palo Alto brothers to Elko and got a job at the Spanish Ranch.

Range fences were unheard of in those days, but the Spanish Ranch had a unique method of protecting its range from the outside, and also kept their own stock from straying. Their enormous bands of sheep were never grazed on the ranch proper. They were grazed on the outer edges. By constantly circling the ranch the sheep left a swath a mile wide completely devoid of vegetation. Not only did they devour every blade of grass, but their hooves played havoc with the grass roots. The barren space left in their wake, served the purpose nicely. The cattle and horses would graze up to the barren space and turn back.

Pete hadn't been at the ranch long before learning that the main hacienda was a haven for the big time gamblers of San Francisco. Pedro and Bernard were good hosts and easy marks for the professional gamblers from the big city. Most everyone who worked at the ranch gambled and drank. Even the sheepherders came in from the range to be sheared of their meager earnings. Consequently, from neglect, the sheep were dying of liver flukes, a disease spread by buzzards.

The ranch owners, knowing that the Basques were fine shepherds, and that Pete was an experienced sheepherder, offered to put him in charge of all of their sheep on a partnership basis. This meant he would share in the profits from the sale of the wool and the mutton. Pete turned the offer down, which he later regretted, knowing that he had passed up an opportunity to make a fortune.

A Scottish widow with three daughters lived between Elko and Cherry Creek. The family was struggling to make a living on a small ranch. The struggle was hard at times, but due to thrift and with the aid of a hired man they managed to eke out a living. It so happened when Pete left the employ of the Spanish Ranch, the Scotch lassies were in need of a hired man and he got the job. Being conscientious and hard working, he was soon enfolded into the family life. During the long winter evenings the girls taught him to read and write English, for which he was forever grateful, as that was the only schooling he ever received in this country. Pete's penmanship was good and he was well versed in world affairs.

Romance began to creep into Pete's life for the second time. He was falling in love with his youngest tutor. Then he thought of Rosa, the girl who had jilted him in Madera. Having been burned once was enough for him, he knew it was time to move on.

Pete was now 26 years old. He had been in America 10 years and had held a variety of jobs, none of which paid very much. The next two jobs didn't pay much either, but they had the distinction of being the coldest jobs he ever had. There are a few places in Nevada, in the high country, where in severe winters the temperature drops to 40° below zero. It was this kind of a winter when Pete took a job herding sheep at Fish Creek for Claude Ford, whose son, J. M. Ford, many years later, was to become a member of the Inyo County Board of Supervisors. The whole countryside was covered with ice and snow. Raging blizzards swept through the mountains and across the high tablelands. The cold wind chilled the marrow in a man's bones. When Pete and the sheep were on the move, the cold to some extent was bearable. But at night when the sheep bedded down, their fleece froze to the ice and they couldn't move. To prevent them from freezing to death, and many did, they had to be chopped free from the ice with an axe. This was tedious and dangerously hard work, when coupled with the severity of the cold. Pete became ill with pneumonia and had to be removed from the job.

When he recovered from his bout with pneumonia he went down to Eureka in search of another job. Eureka was a thriving frontier town, the terminal of a branch line railroad that tied up with the mainline railroad to the north at Palisade. Pete had no trouble in obtaining a job as a stage driver with the Clendenning Stage Company, whose line operated between Eureka and Ely. It was still winter and still cold, with blizzards raging across the desolate mountain pass which the stage traversed. Pete often wondered why he had taken the job; but a fellow had to eat, which he meant to do as long as he could keep from freezing to death.

Normally, four horses were used to pull the stage, but when the snow drifted and banked high on the road it was necessary to use six. The U.S. Mail had to go through as long as it was humanly possible. There were times when Pete had reason to believe that it wasn't going to be humanly possible for the mail to go through. Sometimes the struggling horses with six inch icicles hanging from their nostrils, would flounder in the deep snow drifts. When this happened at night, it was rough. Pete would get out the long-handled shovel and, by the light of a flickering lantern, attack the snow bank. Sometimes he shoveled for hours to open the road.

Pete's run was from Eureka to Hamilton, then a famous silver mining camp but a ghost town today. Another driver with a fresh team would take the stage from Hamilton to Ely. Late one evening when the stage pulled out of Eureka, there were only two passengers aboard, a couple of miners who were returning to their job at a mine near Hamilton. From their appearance and actions, Pete knew that they had been on a typical miner's spree. He was right, for the boys were still high in spirit and getting higher all the time as they had brought along a jug of liquor and a guitar.

At first they did not notice the cold, being busily engaged in serenading Pete with ribald songs.

As the evening wore into night and the rolling wheels crunched out mile after mile over the frozen snow, their revelry began to abate somewhat. The jug was empty and their high spirits were vanishing rapidly. It was then they began to notice the bitter cold. As the alcohol gradually died out of their systems, they began to freeze. Waving their arms around like windmills and stomping their feet to keep up circulation, they began to grumble, then complain, and finally to curse. Engaging Pete in conversation, they told him what they thought about everything in general, but the main theme was the blasted cold they were having to endure. They told him he must be crazy to hold down such a cold job. He told them that he did not like the job but he had to eat. When they learned what a small salary he received, they were downright sorry for him, and wanted to do him a favor by getting him a job in the warm mine where they worked. They did him a favor all right, for he quit the stage line and went to work in the mine. A few days later the mine closed down and Pete was back in the cold, without a job.

CHAPTER VI

GAMBLING FEVER

In the year 1900, big black-mustached Jim Butler was appointed Prosecutor of Nye County, Nevada, by the governor. Butler was a big easy-going man with broad shoulders and a ready smile. He was a rancher, part-time prospector, and a miner and he had no legal training whatsoever. The District Attorney of Nevada at the time was Tasker L. Oddie, a young lawyer from New Jersey, who later became United States Senator Oddie of Nevada. Butler saw in young Oddie, a thoroughly trained lawyer, a way to hold onto his post and whatever political influence it brought him. He seized upon the opportunity and appointed Oddie to act as prosecutor while he retained the title.

One day Butler brought in several pieces of quartz, which he said he had found near a place the Indians called Tonopah (Little Water). He had accidentally stumbled upon the outcropping while hunting a strayed burro. Butler who believed the region to be rich in silver, took the quartz to Frank Hicks, the assayer. Hicks refused to do the assaying because Butler already owed him for four previous assay jobs. Butler then gave the quartz to Oddie and asked him to have it assayed. Oddie promised to have it done. Meanwhile, Butler told Oddie that if the ore panned out good, he would give him a third interest in the property. Oddie was broke at the time so he sent the samples to his friend Walter Gayhart, the school superintendent in Austin. Gayhart was also an assayer. Oddie wrote Gayhart that he was not able to pay for his services, but that if the ore was any good he would give him a half-interest in the third he had been promised by Butler. When Gayhart assayed the samples he could hardly believe his eyes when he saw the size of the silver buttons which came from the crucibles. The ore was rich beyond belief. When Oddie received the astounding report, he immediately sent for Butler, to whom he broke the news.

Butler was not greatly impressed, for he was busy at the time cutting his hay crop and that had to be finished before taking on a new project. Oddie tauntingly told him, "You'd cut a hundred dollar hay crop before you would stake out claims which might be worth a hundred times more than your whole ranch?" When they finally got around to staking the claims, Mrs. Butler was brought in as a partner. When they mined the first load of ore they did not have a team and wagon in which to haul it to the railroad to be shipped to the smelter, and as a result they were forced to take in another partner, Wilson Brougher, who was able to supply a team and wagon. This made five partners, which later caused much litigation when the claims proved to be fabulously rich. The first load of ore shipped ran $800 a ton. That's how Tonopah was born, its mines second only to Virginia City as producers of wealth in Nevada.

While all this was going on, Pete was working at a mine near Butler's ranch at Warm Springs. He was well acquainted with Butler, having worked with him at the Klondike Mine near Eureka. Pete went to Tonopah early in 1901, where he stayed until the fall of 1902. When he arrived, the boom was in full swing. Quite a town had mushroomed up in less than a year. Pete was Tonopah's first ice deliveryman. The ice was hauled in by stage from Candelaria and sold for 30¢ a pound. His second job was that of a water hauler. The water was hauled by wagon and team from springs and wells six miles west of town. The water sold for $4 a barrel, which was more than the cost of a barrel of wine in France. When Pete quit the job, he had to resort to the use of his fists to collect his wages.

He was working for a man named Sinclair and his job as a water hauler lasted only 20 days. One morning he was having trouble with the jack while trying to grease the wagon axles. Sinclair came out with a nasty hangover and started giving Pete a bad time about how to use a wagon jack. Pete retorted that the jack was worn out and Sinclair began cursing him. Pete was already soured on the job so he told Sinclair to go to hell and quit. His wages were $5 a day which meant he had $100 coming. He told Sinclair he wanted his money. Sinclair replied that he would give him a punch in the nose. Pete said, "Never mind the punch in the nose, just give me my money." Sinclair climbed on the wagon and drove away with Pete following in fast pursuit. Sinclair stopped in front of a saloon a couple blocks down the street and Pete repeated the request for his wages. Again, Sinclair told him that he would punch him in the nose. Hurriedly, wrapping the reins around the brake handle, Sinclair jumped off the wagon and swung at Pete. Pete took the blow on his shoulder and hit Sinclair a mighty wallop on the chin, knocking him out cold. An old fellow who was swamping out the saloon was watching the fracas. Shuffling back in the saloon he came out with a sprinkling can and poured water on Sinclair who was lying in the dusty street. The owner of the saloon arrived on the scene and wanted to know what the trouble was about. Pete enlightened him. Regaining consciousness, Sinclair sat up, looked around in a dazed manner and asked what had happened. The saloon-keeper asked him why he hadn't paid Pete. Sinclair said that he did not have the money and asked for a loan. They all tramped into the saloon and the saloon-keeper obliged him with the loan, as he was a Sinclair water customer. To show his appreciation, Pete bought a round of drinks for the house. The miners coming off the graveyard shift had begun to drift into the saloon. One round of drinks called for another and another and before Pete left the saloon he had spent more than $60.

George Tibo, a man Pete knew quite well, owned a ranch at Warm Springs. When the strike was made at Tonopah, Tibo sold the ranch and went to Tonopah where he built and operated a store and a rooming house. Pete was rooming with Tibo and for safekeeping, Tibo permitted him to keep his money in the store safe. One night before bedtime Pete went across the street to the Bower Saloon to have a nightcap. Pete wasn't much of a gambler, but he got interested in watching a young fellow bucking the roulette wheel. The young fellow was winning as evidenced by the pile of money in front of him. This fascinated Pete, and having a $5 bill in his pocket, he decided to try his luck.

The houseman changed the five for him and, "By gee," he lost $4 in four plays. With the last dollar he played 50¢ each on No. 17 and No. 20. Seventeen came up and he collected $17.50. He began playing silver dollars on several different numbers. His luck was good from then on and he and the young fellow broke the bank twice, whereupon the dealer closed the game. Pete won $1700 and the other fellow had won much more. His winnings were mostly $20 gold pieces, which were almost as plentiful as silver dollars in Tonopah in those days. Pete started for his room with the gold dragging heavily in his pockets. He had the key in the door when gambling fever and beginner's luck took over. He just couldn't resist the temptation to go back and win more money.

Yes! he was going to break every roulette bank in Tonopah. Feeling big, he entered the Hanksite Saloon, strolled up to the roulette table and placed a silver dollar on a number. The house-man stopped the wheel saying, "Sorry buddy, you can only play a quarter here." Acting like a big gambler, Pete replied, "What's the matter? They're playing dollars across the street?" "A quarter is our limit," the houseman told him. One word led to another and finally the houseman called the manager over and told him that Pete wanted to play a dollar. Sizing Pete up, the manager figured him for a "greenie," and said, "Let him play a dollar." Pete played his dollar all right. Many, many dollars later, he happened to look up and was surprised to see it was daylight. He had lost $1,400, and only $300 of his winnings remained in his pocket. That night he was back in the saloon determined to win back the $1,400.

Three nights later his last dollar was raked in by the dealer in the Tonopah Club. Not only had he lost what he had won in the beginning but also his $700 savings out of Mr. Tibo's safe was gone too. The dealer, knowing that Pete was broke, tossed him a couple of dollars to eat on. Pete immediately placed the $2 on a number. "Oh, no, I gave you that to eat on," said the dealer. "You can't play it here." Pete became angry, shoving the money back to the dealer; he told him to go to hell, and walked out.

The three day gambling spree had cost him all of his savings and his job as well. He was thoroughly disgusted with himself. Being too proud to beg or borrow, he went without food for three days while searching for a job. On the third day he was suffering from hunger pangs and getting weaker by the moment. As he walked along the street, he passed a store owned by a Jew. The Jew called to him and asked if he wanted a job. These were the magic words he had been waiting to hear. "You betcha, what you want me to do?" he asked. There was a cellar under the store where the rain water had seeped through the soil, filling the cellar with a foot of water. The job was to bail out the water. Before it was finished he was so near exhaustion he could hardly lift the last few buckets. The Jew paid him $3 for the work. Pete staggered down the street to a Chinese restaurant where he could get all he could eat for 50¢. He ordered a big meal but when the food was placed in front of him he became nauseated and couldn't eat. Forcing himself to stay, he managed to get some liquids down and after awhile he was able to eat.

Later in the day he was hired by a man named McNamara, who owned and operated a slaughter house and butcher shop. The job was to help drive cattle from Bishop, California, to Tonopah. Next morning he was at the slaughter house in time to have breakfast with the cowpunchers before starting on horseback to Bishop. The cowpunchers were having beefsteak for breakfast. Pete's appetite had returned and how he ate, filling up on two steaks! The drive from Bishop with the cattle took about 10 days and he then punched the cattle in the hills around Tonopah while they waited to be slaughtered. Later he worked in the slaughterhouse making sausage and from there was promoted to the butcher shop. McNamara was interested in the mining game, as was everyone else in Tonopah at the time. He owned three claims near Lone Mountain. Knowing that Pete had some mining experience, he sent him out in two feet of snow to help drive a tunnel on the claims. It was here that Pete heard about the gold strike in Goldfield. Quitting the job he pulled out for the new strike.

Al Meyers, who had made the original Goldfield strike, was hauling a load of lumber from Tonopah down to Goldfield. Pete threw his tent and bedroll on the wagon and rode down with Meyers. Meyers went on to become a prominent and wealthy man in western Nevada and eastern California mining circles. He lived to a ripe old age and at the time of his death in Tujunga, California, he owned several of the famous old silver mines at Panamint City.

Pete was the fifth man to arrive in Goldfield in the winter of 1902. The Goldfield boom turned out to be as large as the Tonopah boom. At the start a few people said that Goldfield would never amount to anything, but in 1906 there were 60,000 people in Goldfield. The Goldfield mines produced more gold in the short time they lasted, than any other mines in the Union. Some idea of the wealth produced by the mines is gleaned from the fact that they paid $25 million in dividends to stockholders. When Pete arrived in Goldfield he pitched his tent at what later turned out to be the heart of town and went to work helping develop the January Mine. Being the fifth man to arrive on the scene of the strike, he passed up a golden opportunity to stake good claims, which could have made him a wealthy man.

Pete worked as an ore sorter for more than a year at the January Mine. January Jones and Shorty Cantill taught him how to distinguish gold bearing quartz from waste rock. It was while working at the January Mine that he got the prospecting fever. A prospector had made a strike at Montezuma, eight miles east of Goldfield, and had brought some high-grade gold ore samples to the Oly Elliot Saloon. When Pete saw the samples he decided to go to the scene of the new strike and stake his first mining claim. Arising early the next morning he rode out to the new strike with a French Canadian wood hauler. Arriving on the scene he found the hills literally covered with people. Going to a few he asked where the strike was. He was told that he was walking over it, but that he was too late as all the good ground had been staked.

Wandering to the outer edge of activity, he found a likely looking outcropping where he staked a claim and built monuments. Knocking off about 25 pounds of rock for samples he placed them in an ore sack and packed them on his back the eight miles to Goldfield. Enroute he met Tom Murphy and his partner, who were headed for the strike and he showed them his samples. Murphy told him the samples were nothing but iron pyrite which bears a striking resemblence to gold. Pete, being a suspicious Basque, did not believe him. He thought perhaps Murphy was pulling his leg. Packing the samples on to Goldfield, he had them assayed. Murphy had been right, they ran only $1 a ton in gold. Pete decided then and there that he had better further his education in distinguishing gold bearing rock, so he went back to work as an ore sorter at the January Mine.

By now there were several thousand people in Goldfield and a man named Booth had surveyed the townsite. Pete's tent was right in the middle of Main Street. Arriving home from work one night he found a note from Booth telling him to move the tent out of the street. By then all the lots had been taken or sold and if he moved he would have to move clear out of town. He went to see Booth, who adamantly demanded that he clear his tent off the street. Pete was just as adamant, and he continued to live in the middle of the street. Teams and wagons ran over the tent guy ropes and many times the tent was knocked down. Finally he built a fence around the tent and lived in it until April 1905. At one time he was offered $500 for his home in the middle of the street.

Pete recalled that he saw his first automobile in Goldfield in 1905. It was a gala event. All morning the streets were thronged with people waiting for a glimpse of the horseless carriage. The automobile belonged to and was driven into Goldfield by Sherwood Aldrich.

Labor trouble began to boil up in Goldfield and when violence started, Pete decided it was time to go prospecting. It was spring and the wide open desert was calling. He had money in the bank, more than enough to purchase his own outfit, but it was customary to have a grubstaking partner or two to provide the necessary supplies and equipment. In return for the grubstake, they would benefit from any worthwhile claims the prospector might locate.

Frank Flynn, a ranch owner in Ruby Valley, and Tom Kavanagh, a restauranteur in Goldfield, grubstaked Pete, even furnishing him with a string of four burros. The boom was moving southward toward the Death Valley country. Strikes had already been made at Bullfrog, Rhyolite, Greenwater, Keane Wonder and in the Panamint Mountains near Ballarat. Pete headed south, leisurely prospecting the hills toward the Bullfrog District and Rhyolite coming out of the hills at old man Beatty's ranch. The ranch was on the Amargosa River just east of what is now the town of Beatty, which bears his name. Beatty lived in true frontier style, surrounded by his squaw and family of halfbreeds. He harbored the wayfarers who, at times, disturbed his monotonous existence.

CHAPTER VII

STALKED *by the* GRIM REAPER

RHYOLITE

Stretched across the ivoried sticks of a fan
Are the scenes of another day
Quaintly reminiscent of chivalry and romance
Softly mournful in memory of red-gold nights.
The silken fabric is broken by time.
Parted to separate yesterday from today
And fragrant as a rose of yesterday
The pungent sagebrush comes across this fan,
A dull reminder that memory alone remains
To mock the fragrance of departed yesterdays.
— James Neill Northe

Life began for the Bullfrog, Nevada Mining District and Rhyolite on August 9, 1904, the day Ed Cross struck a boulder of quartz with his pick and brought to light virgin gold literally sprinkled throughout the green-stained rock which reminded Cross of a bullfrog. Shorty Harris was along when Ed Cross discovered the Bullfrog Mine, so naturally Shorty claimed credit for the discovery.

From Ed Cross' strike, Rhyolite blossomed into a town of 10,000 people, with gambling houses, a redlight district, 57 saloons, churches, a school, a hospital, the *Rhyolite Herald* newspaper, a bottle house (built with 51,000 beer bottles at a cost of $25,000), a fire department, whose equipment was pulled by the firemen, and tents, shacks and houses of all sizes and description. A magnificent Union Station serviced three railroads, the Tonopah and Tidewater, the Bullfrog-Goldfield and the Las Vegas-Tonopah. All this comprised the booming town. Rhyolite weathered the money panic of 1907. The years from 1906 through 1909 were the boom years. By 1911 the town had begun to return to sagebrush and sand.

Today, all that remains intact is the bottle house, which contains a desert museum founded by Bill Murphy, and the magnificent depot which Wes Westmoreland converted into a palatial casino and saloon with guest rooms upstairs. Standing as a monument among the ruins of the once proud town are the walls of the three-storied John S. Cook Company's $90,000 building which is located at what was once the corner of Golden Street and Broadway. This building housed the First National Bank of Rhyolite and the post office. Other forlorn ruins are the walls of the Porter Brothers Store. The two brothers had come over from Ballarat where they had owned and operated a store.

When Pete reached Rhyolite in the spring of 1905, the town was in its infancy. There was quite a bit of excitement over the amount of blasting that was heard in the hills surrounding the town. One was led to believe that a big boom was in progress, with a lot of mining being done. Pete met Julian Ubner, a fellow whom he knew, and he asked him what all the blasting was about. Ubner laughingly told him that a few mining promoters were in town and that most every person who had claims for sale, had grabbed powder and fuse, high-tailed it to their claims and were blasting away, trying to impress the mining promotors. Ubner gave Pete a fraction of a claim that he owned adjacent to the Mayflower property. After looking it over, Pete decided it was worthless and let it go. A few months later when the Mayflower Mine started operation, another fellow sold the fraction that Pete thought worthless for $6,000. A prospector's luck.

Pete was anxious to be on with his prospecting, so he didn't tarry long in Rhyolite. Packing his burros, he pulled out heading for Forty Mile Canyon, which, he had been told, was virgin country for prospecting. As he went over the saucer-shaped rim above Rhyolite, he took one last look at the sprawling mining camp, little realizing that on December 6, 1906, he would be standing in the 66 Saloon across the street from the telegraph office, awaiting the arrival of a message that would tell him his interest in some mining claims had been purchased by a mining syndicate for $60,000.

When Pete got into Forty Mile Canyon, the country looked good to him. He prospected the canyon clear to the head and swung east, crossing a large playa to the foothills beyond. He planned on prospecting the hills for a few days and then to head back for Beatty's ranch. This was waterless country, his water supply was running low and the summer heat had begun to bear down. In those days there were no maps of this desolate country and very few, if any, of the landmarks bore names. There might have been isolated springs in the area but Pete never found any of them. The only water he knew of was back at Beatty's ranch, which was 40 miles or more away. One morning he inventoried his water supply and found that he had enough for one more day in camp and enough to take him safely back to the Beatty Ranch. That afternoon he saw what looked to be a promising outcropping up on the side of a mountain. He went up to investigate. When he returned to camp with an empty canteen, he found the burros gone and the camp in a sad state of chaos. Before departing, the burros had looted the food box, consuming everything that was edible. The bag of flour was torn and scattered over the ground and the camp looked as if it were covered with snow. Losing the food was bad enough but the real tragedy was that the burros had pawed holes in the water cans and all the water was gone.

Pete knew he was in a tough spot. He was forty miles from water and the weather was hot. He took it as calmly as possible. Gathering up a few things that could be carried easily, including the gold pan, his gun and some salt, he started out hunting the burros. He hunted them all night and half the next day before finding them. By this time he was suffering so from thirst that he had almost reached the limit of his endurance. Self-preservation was the strongest thing in his mind at the time and he grasped the last straw by shooting one of the burros. Cutting its jugular vein, he caught the blood in his gold pan. Drinking enough to alleviate his thirst, he added salt to the remainder, stirring it so it would not curdle, and poured it into his canteen.

Fortunately the burros had strayed in the direction of Beatty's ranch. Now that he could ride his saddle burro, he felt confident that he would come out safely, knowing that if he ran out of liquid he could kill another burro. He reached the springs at Beatty's ranch before he had to do this.

Looking back on this near-tragedy, he said it was the closest call he ever had, excepting perhaps the time he was overcome by Death Valley heat while attempting a crossing in June with his burros, or when a fellow at Harrisburg Flat shot him and the bullet glanced off his head, leaving a small crack in his skull.

Pete returned to Rhyolite where he rested for a few days and reoutfitted. He decided to cross Death Valley and prospect for the rest of the summer in the high Panamint Mountains where the weather was cool. Before leaving Rhyolite, he was warned by other prospectors not to attempt to cross Death Valley in the summer heat; that if he did, his bones would be found the following winter.

Pete was 31 years old at the time. Just in his prime and as tough as old boot leather. He laughed at them and vowed that when he returned to Rhyolite he would be the owner of a rich mine. He lived up to the promise, for when he returned to Rhyolite that winter he owned an interest in some claims that would turn into a good gold mine. But their prophecy about his dying almost came true as the terrible summer heat in Death Valley all but claimed him for another victim.

Leaving Rhyolite, Pete headed out over Daylight Pass where he had the Death Valley scene before him all afternoon. As he wended his way in a circuitous manner down the steep slope of the Funeral Mountains, the valley before him was engulfed with thick blue heat that continually rose from its desolate bottom. He imagined that he was looking into a region of Hades with the lid off.

This was the valley of death, with many victims to its credit. Tomesha (ground afire) was what the Indians called it, and tomorrow he was going to attempt to cross this valley. It might be a foolish thing to do, but there was no turning back now.

As Pete and his burros plodded along down the mountain, one of the burros bumped a protruding boulder with its pack and fell from the narrow trail. The burro rolled over and over for several hundred feet, landing at the bottom of the canyon. Pete thought for sure that it would be killed by the fall but it jumped to its feet and shook itself as though nothing had happened. A burro is one of the toughest animals known to man and they are about the hardest thing in the world to kill. They can take a lot of punishment and still come back for more. Fortunately, Pete's bedding was lashed on top of the burro's pack and none of the supplies were damaged by the fall. Getting the burro back on the trail was quite a problem, but he finally made it and continued on down the trail.

It was mid-afternoon when he sighted a group of tents pitched far below in the recess of a canyon which lay to the left. Somehow he had missed the turn-off trail that led to Keane Spring and what he saw below was the Keane-Wonder Mine Camp. He hoped that he would be able to replenish his water supply there. The Keane-Wonder Mine had been discovered in 1902 by Jack Keane and Domingo Etcharren. Pete knew Etcharren, a Basque, who had come from his home town in Mauleon, France, in the Pyrenees Mountains.

Pete arrived at the mine first, as the camp was further down the trail. The mine consisted of a series of tunnels in the canyon wall. Not receiving an answer to his calls, he penetrated the tunnels as far as he dared without a light and soon discovered that the mine was not being worked at the time. Going on down to the camp he found it abandoned too. There were six tents, a barn and a galvanized water tank which was empty. It was a dry camp as there was no spring. Later he learned that water used at the mine and camp had to be packed for a distance of seven miles by burro train from the Keane Spring, which was at a higher elevation in another canyon. He also learned that due to the Death Valley heat the mine was only worked during the winter months and that it had been abandoned since the first of March.

Pete's water cans were half empty. He wasn't about to start across Death Valley without a full supply of water; he was going to have to back-track up the mountain, find Keane Spring and replenish the supply.

Before turning back, he went on down the canyon and found two more tents. A dead dog lay by the side of one of them. He recognized the dog as one belonging to a Mr. Young whom he had met in Rhyolite. So this was Mr. Young's camp? But where was Mr. Young? He was almost afraid to look. After making a thorough search and not finding any signs of life and as it was getting late, he turned back up the trail to the Keane-Wonder Camp, where he bedded down alongside the barn.

Due to the heat Pete had lost his appetite, so he did not prepare an evening meal. Turning the burros loose he spread his blankets on the ground and turned in. There was something eerie about the place that made him uneasy and it was a long time before he fell asleep. Subconsciously sensing that something was wrong, he awoke with a start. Everything was too quiet. For a moment or two he could not understand why. Arising to investigate, he found that the burros were gone. Thinking perhaps they had not strayed far, he started tracking them by moonlight. The tracks led down the canyon toward Death Valley. He tracked the burros clear to the floor of the valley before finding them.

It was near daylight when he got back to camp, tired and thirsty. After resting for awhile he cooked breakfast then broke camp, packed the burros and headed back up the mountain, hoping to find Keane Spring without further trouble. But he again took the wrong trail and wound up in a blind canyon at what proved to be Dan Driscoll's mining camp. Dan was gone for the summer. Here, Pete encountered two men who were also searching for the spring. Fortunately, there was water left in Driscoll's tank from which they filled their containers. The two strangers were the first persons Pete had seen in three days. He remembered part of the conversation they had. As he approached the camp and before they could see him, one called out, "Who's there?" To which Pete replied, "A friend." Then one asked, "Lost too, are you?" and Pete replied, "I'm not lost, I'm looking for Keane Spring." "Well, we're in the same boat, we're looking for the spring too, but its not here. However, we have found water in the tank."

As was the custom of the day, no introductions were made. After they had talked for awhile, Pete told them of his intentions to cross Death Valley alone that night. The spokesman for the two, with a quick flash of the eyes and in a husky voice said, "I would not let a dog, let alone a man, attempt that hazardous trip in the night. I would shoot him down first." While he had put it in a generally diplomatic way for a man of the desert and mountains, he could not have drawn a bead on Pete with his gun and commanded him directly not to go to impress it more plainly. Pete decided in a hurry to camp with them for the night.

The next morning found them up long before dawn. After participating in a hurriedly prepared breakfast of flapjacks, bacon and coffee, he bid the two men goodbye as if they were old friends and took off down the mountain. He learned afterwards that when the two men returned to Rhyolite and told a group of acquaintances about a crazy Frenchman they had met in the Funeral Mountains who was going to cross Death Valley alone in the summer heat, more than one prayer was offered in his behalf.

Pete had been told about a well that contained brackish water at the edge of the valley. Although the water was unfit to drink, in an emergency it could be used to a good advantage in moistening one's body. He did not find the well.

Knowing that he stood a better chance with less discomfort in crossing Death Valley at night, he tarried along the trail until the burning sun disappeared behind the Panamint Mountains and then struck out. He was not following a trail and along about midnight one of the burros mired down to its belly in a salt marsh. It seemed that he worked for hours trying to free the burro. Finally by using pack ropes and other burros to pull, he was able to release it from the marsh. Backtracking for a distance, he turned south toward Greenland Ranch (now Furnace Creek Ranch.) If he had only turned north, within a few miles he would have struck the well worn trail which led to Stovepipe Wells and Emigrant Springs in Emigrant Wash.

Morning came and with it came the sun, a red ball of fire that rose from behind the Funeral Mountains, and the heat began to bear down in earnest. As the day wore on, a heat mirage caused Greenland Ranch to loom up as if it were only a mile or two away. But as he rode along on the saddle burro, he did not seem to come any closer to the ranch.

The heat was becoming unbearable. He was constantly moistening his lips with his tongue and taking sips of water, which was now hot from the canteen. He knew that he had to use caution in conserving the water. The dry, hot air was sapping his body of its moisture. He wasn't conscious of perspiring as the heat was licking it up before it reached the surface of the skin. Even the moisture in his eyes was drying up, making it difficult to keep them open. His body was rapidly dehydrating. He encountered no wildlife whatever, no insects or flies bothered him. The valley floor, far below sea level, was devoid of vegetation. Once he got off the burro to seek relief in the shade of a rock. He lay on his back and watched a golden eagle soar out from Telescope Peak as if to cross the valley. Half-way across it circled and turned back to the cool sanctuary of the mountains.

As he rode along he came to a newly-made grave, which contained the earthly remains of Tim Ryan (the camp at the borax mine in Death Valley bears his name), an oldtime prospector who had succumbed to the heat a few days before and had been buried on the spot where his body was found. If Pete had harbored sufficient energy, he would have dismounted, kneeled by the side of the grave, and prayed to the Lord to save him from the fate of Tim Ryan.

The burros were standing the heat better than he was as they monotonously plodded along. Encountering a stream of salt water he thought that if he got into the water and took a bath he would feel better. He removed his boots and clothing and with the ground blistering the bottom of his feet, causing him to hurry, he slipped into the stream. The water scalded him. He scramblbed out and struggled into his clothing. The metal buttons on his overalls were so hot, that when accidently touched by the back of his hand, they would burn the skin. The sun had already blistered the top of his feet through the heavy leather miner's boots he wore.

He began to have dizzy spells, everything would turn black and he would have to cling to the saddlehorn to keep from falling from the burro. The ranch seemed so close at times that he could almost reach out and touch it, yet it was miles away. As he swayed dizzily in the saddle he clung to the burro with what little strength he had left. Night finally came as the burros plodded silently on. He knew if he could manage to stay aboard the burro, it would save his life.

Arousing from a stupor he heard a dog barking and he knew he had reached the ranch safely. A silent prayer formed on his lips.

CHAPTER VIII

DEATH VALLEY SCOTTY

When Pete arrived at the ranch and fell from the burro, he was more dead than alive. He was placed under the skillful care of Oscar Denton, caretaker and foreman of the ranch, and the Indians who were employed on the ranch, and they had him back on his feet in a couple of days. This was not the first "greenie" they had saved from the clutches of Death Valley.

Pete owed his life to the faithful burro, for if he had been afoot he would never have reached the ranch. His body, or bones, would have been found like many others, with arms outstretched toward the ranch, as if in their dying struggle they were reaching for its life saving shade and water, which was so close, yet so far.

Denton was raising alfalfa and figs with Indian labor. The Indians, wise in the ways of self-preservation in the deadly heat, only worked the ranch from daylight to sunup and from sundown to dark.

The highest official temperature ever recorded in Death Valley was 134° in the year 1913. In later years, Pete often wondered if it was that hot when the valley almost claimed him as a victim.

Greenland Ranch was first known as Borax Smith's Ranch. A veritable desert oasis, it was fed by the potable water from a creek which flows from the Funeral Mountains. Before the coming of Borax Smith, the oasis was inhabited for years, probably centuries, by the Shoshone Indians.

Before the turn of the century, Borax Smith used the ranch as a watering and feeding place for his stock and a resting place for the weary teamsters who were hauling borax out of Death Valley with 18-mule teams. Today, modern travelers may see one of the giant borax wagons standing in front of Furnace Creek Ranch, a monument to Borax Smith, the man who pioneered borax mining in Death Valley country. Due to the water, trees and grass at the ranch, the temperature is usually eight to ten degrees cooler than the rest of the valley.

The tragedy that befell James "Jimmy" W. Dayton, age 62, in 1899, probably drew the first big-time publicity to the ranch. Dayton had weathered out 15 blistering summers as caretaker and foreman at the ranch. He hauled his supplies out of Daggett. As a safety measure in the summer time, he would write ahead and inform the storekeeper to expect him on or near a certain date. In the last days of July, he started for Daggett by wagon and team. When he failed to arrive on time, the storekeeper sent Frank Tilton and Adolph Navares in search of him. In the deadly heat near Bennett Wells they found the remains of Jimmy Dayton beneath a mesquite. Dayton, before crawling off the wagon, had set the brake, and the horses unable to move the wagon had died in harness. Only his dog had survived and it had beaten a pathway from the wagon to its master and was guarding the body with the little strength he had left.

Tilton and Navares buried Dayton on the spot, and today, the grave of Frank "Shorty" Harris lies beside it. Above Harris' and Dayton's grave a bronze plaque in a rock monument bears the following inscription:

"BURY ME BESIDE JIM DAYTON IN THE
VALLEY WE LOVED. ABOVE ME WRITE:
'HERE LIES SHORTY HARRIS, A SINGLE
BLANKET JACKASS PROSPECTOR."—EPITAPH
REQUESTED BY SHORTY (FRANK) HARRIS
BELOVED GOLD HUNTER. 1856-1934.
HERE JAS. DAYTON, PIONEER, PERISHED, 1898.

TO THESE TRAILMAKERS WHOSE COURAGE MATCHED
THE DANGERS OF THE LAND, THIS BIT OF EARTH
IS DEDICATED FOREVER.

There is a discrepancy in the year of Dayton's death. W. A. Chalfant, dean of Death Valley writers, in his book, *Death Valley —The Facts*, stated the year was 1899, while the date on the plaque is 1898.

It was while recuperating at the ranch that Pete heard the story about the miner who was working the graveyard shift at the Skeleton Mine near Tombstone Flat in Coffin Canyon in the Funeral Mountains overlooking Death Valley.

During his stay at the Ranch, Pete met "Death Valley Scotty" for the first time. He was known then as "Mysterious Scott". Scott boarded a change of burros at the ranch. He would arrive early in the morning, sleep most of the day, then switch his packs to fresh burros and leave at dark.

Pete found Scotty a congenial person with personality plus, who liked to talk about himself and everything else but never about the exact location of the secret gold mine which he was supposed to have someplace in Death Valley.

Pete knew Death Valley Scotty for 40 years. He always said that Scotty's gold mine was his personality and salesmanship; that he could have sold iceboxes to Eskimos. He was a promoter and a showman, the P. T. Barnum of the West. For Scotty there wasn't a sucker born every minute, but there was one born often enough to keep him in folding money.

Many oldtimers in the Death Valley country knocked Scotty. It was a case of jealousy. They said that he was a big bag of wind; that he never owned a producing gold mine. Most of his critics, when they died, were living off the old age pension, while Scotty, when he died on January 5, 1954, was living in a three million dollar castle.

At one time, hanging on the wall in Wildrose Station, there was a gold stock certificate calling for 100 shares of stock at $1 per share, issued by the Death Valley Gold Mining and Developing Company. Scotty's picture, red necktie and all, adorned the upper right hand corner of the imposing gilt-edged certificate. Scotty gave the 100 shares to Clarence Tilson of Bakersfield on May 5, 1913, telling him that it would make him rich.

In 1905, when Pete first met Scotty, there were some who swore that Scotty really did have a rich gold mine.

The morning after Scotty left the ranch, Pete questioned Denton about Scotty and his gold mine. Denton told him that Scotty was a mysterious man who came and went in a haphazard manner. Scotty would disappear for a few days in the Funeral Mountains and when he returned to the ranch the burros would be loaded with sacks of quartz. Pete asked Denton if he had ever seen or panned any of this quartz and got this reply, "Pan it? Hell, you don't have to pan it, it's half gold." Denton also told Pete that Scotty had said more than once that nobody had better ever try to follow him to the mine, for if they did, he might take a shot at them.

Years later when Pete was in the chips he visited Scotty's cabin up near Ubehebe Crater. Scotty wasn't at home, but there was a note tacked on the front door. "Welcome," it said, "If you are hungry help yourself, but be damn sure you wash the dishes." The cabin door was not locked. Pete walked in and found a lot of fancy canned goods on the pantry shelf where he found another note, "Beware of my pet rattlesnake."

Pete met Scotty at the ranch in Death Valley in June, 1905, and in July Scotty chartered a special Santa Fe passenger train and made a record-breaking run from Los Angeles to Chicago.

Many people, unfamiliar with its history, believe Death Valley to be a place where some gold-seeking emigrants died. This conception is false. The Jayhawkers and the Bennett-Arcane parties reached Death Valley near Christmas time in 1849. The climate was ideal, the days in general were warm and sunny and the nights cool and invigorating. It is true, they suffered terrible hardships, for they were lost, hungry, trail weary and short of supplies. The Panamint Mountains blocked further advancement westward toward the gold fields as far as the wagons were concerned. So, they killed some of the oxen and used the fire from the burning wagons to jerk the meat. The remaining oxen were used as pack animals and mounts for the women and children as they struggled through the Panamint Mountains and on to the San Francisquito Ranch north of Los Angeles. Only one man, Old Captain Culverwell, died in Death Valley proper, and he died from exhaustion. As the emigrants pushed on, a man by the name of Fish died near the summit of the Slate Range Mountains, and another, William Robinson died further on and a few more were lost as they fanned out and struggled on alone.

The stretch of endless miles over which the emigrants struggled to reach a more hospitable area was much dryer than Death Valley itself.

If the emigrants had been trapped in Death Valley in the summertime, perhaps they all would have died. Some 50 persons have perished in Death Valley since the turn of the century. Many of them died between 1905 and 1910, while trying to cross the valley from the east in the summer enroute to the mining booms at Harrisburg and Skidoo in the Panamint Mountains.

Clark Mills and the writer once crossed Death Valley in mid-afternoon in August (before car air-conditioning). We found it was 116° in the shade at Furnace Creek Ranch. At Stove Pipe Wells it was 121° in the dining room with all the windows open. All metal parts of the automobile were untouchable, even the plastic steering wheel was so hot the driver had to change hands frequently. As we drove rapidly along, I visualized Pete Aguereberry and his burros plodding along in the valley back in the summer of 1905. In my mind I relived his harrowing experience. What suffering he must have endured. I thought about the 134 degree temperature that had been recorded in 1913, and then I thought about the terrible trials of a man and his burro in the early days.

Pete had fully recovered from his brush with death. Now it was time for him to travel on to his original destination, the Panamint Mountains and Ballarat. He was preparing to leave the ranch when word was brought in that two men, Hicks and Levit, had found gold in nearby Echo Canyon in the Funeral Mountains, so Pete headed his burros east toward the site of the new strike. When he arrived at the scene he met Hicks and Levit. Hicks was a big powerful man with a bad reputation. He resented Pete's presence and right away began making trouble. He called Pete a "Dago" and ordered him off what he said were his claims. Pete was a peaceful man, so he ignored the insult. Apologizing for trespassing he started to leave.

Hicks called him back and claimed the burro he was riding. At first, Pete thought he was joking, but when he accused him of having stolen the burro from him, that was too much. Pete had never seen Hicks before and he became furious, telling Hicks that his grubstakers had furnished the burro when they outfitted him in Goldfield. He offered to bet Hicks $100, which he did not have, that the burro did not belong to him. Hicks asked how he could prove that the burro was not his and Pete told him they would go to Goldfield to prove it. Hicks told him they wouldn't go any place and that he was going to take the burro away from him. Pete saw red. There wasn't anyone going to take the burro that had saved his life, unless they killed him first. Pete went for his gun. Levit, who had been listening to the squabble, beat him to the draw. Levelling his gun on Hicks, he said, "Hicks, you know damn well that burro doesn't belong to you. Now cut out the gabbing and get to work." With a look of thanks to Levit, Pete headed his burro train down the canyon.

Two years later Pete met Hicks in Sam Adams' tent saloon at Harrisburg where they were on an equal footing, and asked him if he still thought the burro was his. Hicks apologized and offered to buy him a drink.

Pete camped for the night on the banks of Furnace Creek at the spot where Furnace Creek Inn now stands. A man by the name of Byrne was also camped there. Byrne was headed for Greenwater in the Black Mountains east of Death Valley. Greenwater was a copper boom camp at the time. In the spring of 1904, Arthur Kunze had found a green-stained outcropping and had taken some specimens to Tonopah for assaying. The copper content was high and the boom was on. Greenwater was to be a second Butte, Montana, as a producer of copper, so the promoters said. The multi-millionaire, Charles M. Schwab, must have thought so for he sank half a million dollars in property without getting a cent in return. Byrne, who had visited Greenwater before, tried to persuade Pete to go with him. Pete was reluctant to go as he was almost broke, and then Byrne made the mistake of telling him that Greenwater was a dry camp. He said the nearest water was 40 miles away, and it was hauled by team and wagon, the team consuming half the load on the trip. The half reaching Greenwater sold for 15 cents a gallon, he added. Pete couldn't afford to buy water for himself and the burros and he was tired of chasing someone else's boom. He wanted to create a boom of his own, so he declined to go with Byrne—it was well that he did for Greenwater was a flop that faded in 1907.

The next morning his saddle burro was missing. His first thoughts were that Hicks had taken the burro and when he couldn't find it in the immediate vicinity he became angry as a disturbed hornet. Making for Hicks' and Levit's camp in Echo Canyon, he accused Hicks of taking his burro. Again, level-headed Levit calmed what was rapidly developing into a gun fight, when he intervened by telling Pete that Hicks had not been away from camp and he did not have the burro. Pete returned to his camp on Furnace Creek and he continued to search for the burro. He began to think that prospecting was half burro hunting. He had heard about prospectors finding rich outcroppings while hunting their strayed burros, but no such luck had befallen him.

He was about to give up the search when he met an Indian who could speak English. Describing the burro he asked the Indian if he had seen it. The Indian grunted, "You give me money, I find burro for you." He gave the Indian the last five dollars he had, thinking perhaps he would never see the Indian again. Early next morning the Indian appeared with the burro. Later Pete learned this was the Indian's racket, stealing prospector's burros and conveniently finding them for a fee.

Pete was now broke, his grub was running low and he was a long way from Ballarat where he was to pick up a money order at the post office from his grubstaking partners in Goldfield. Many unforeseen things were to happen to Pete before he reached Ballarat.

CHAPTER IX

EUREKA!

Pete had planned to use the Emigrant Canyon route to Ballarat, but Denton, the ranch foreman, told him about a route which was 30 miles shorter and at a burro's pace of travel, would save him two day's time. The short-cut through Blackwater Canyon was an old Indian trail. There were two trails in the canyon, one wet and one dry. The dry trail was used in wet weather and the wet trail in dry weather. It's hard to visualize anything being wet in Death Valley country, yet, in all the Panamint canyons on the Death Valley side—Emigrant, Blackwater, Trail, Hanaupah, Johnson and Warm Springs—water flows from snow-fed springs through winter and spring months. During the summer and early fall the blazing heat dries up most of the water before it reaches the surface of the ground.

When Pete reached Blackwater Canyon, he found the two trails were badly damaged by a recent cloudburst and were impassable. Setting up a camp, he took his burros back to the ranch. Returning to the canyon, he spent three days repairing the wet trail. His meager supply of grub was about exhausted when he returned to the ranch to get his burros. Here he met Shorty Harris for the first time. Shorty was anxious to go to Ballarat to celebrate the Fourth of July in the boomtown saloons. When he arrived at the ranch, Denton had told him that the trails in Blackwater Canyon were washed out, but that "French Pete" was working the wet trail and that he should have it passable in a day or two. That pleased Shorty for he never had much love for manual labor, and too, it would give him a chance to rest up, and when the Frenchman finished repairing the trail he would still have ample time to reach Ballarat for the Fourth of July celebration. Pete's work on the trail took a day longer than Denton figured, and when Pete returned to the ranch, Shorty was impatient to be on his way. Here it was the last day of June, and he just had to be in Ballarat in time to celebrate the Fourth.

Most prospectors would not cross Death Valley or the Panamint Mountains alone—it was too dangerous. They would camp at a spring and wait for a trail partner to come along. Pete felt honored to travel with Shorty, for Shorty was well known in the Death Valley country as a single-blanket-jackass-prospector, who was supposed to have made several gold strikes. He also knew the trail to Ballarat. Shorty was riding a gray horse and driving four pack burros. Pete was riding a burro and when they broke over the summit of the mountain and started downhill he had trouble keeping up as Shorty was driving his burros at a rapid pace.

Four and a half miles below the summit Pete spied a promising outcropping on the north side of a small hill. Shorty was some distance ahead and he called for him to wait while he investigated the ledge. But Shorty was a man in a hurry and he yelled back, "Holy Smokes, Pete! Fourth of July! Let's get on to Ballarat!" Pete thought, "To hell with him, let him go. I'm here to find gold and all he wants to find is a good time. I'm going to sample that outcropping, it looks good to me." Climbing up on the ledge, the first piece of rock he knocked off was streaked with free-gold. He became greatly excited; this was it, this was what he had been looking for, this was what had almost cost him his life in Death Valley. Gold, Gold, Gold!

As he stood on the wind-swept hill with the gold-bearing rock in his hand, little did he realize that soon 500 men would swarm over the area. Here for years, the Indians and white men had traveled the trail around the hill, little suspecting it was rich with gold. Knocking off a few more pieces of rock and placing them in his sample bag, he hurried down the hill to catch Shorty. His burros had followed Shorty so he was afoot. Anxious to show Shorty the gold he had found, he ran as fast as he could for two miles before overtaking him in Wood Canyon where Shorty was reluctantly waiting. Pete said, "Hi, Shorty, I've got some gold-bearing rock to show you." Shorty, angry by the delay, said, "Ah! to hell with the rocks, they are nothing but lime, schist and shale. Let's go. I've been waiting for two hours for you and we've got 60 miles to go to reach Ballarat." Astounded, Pete said, "Sixty miles? I thought you said it was only 30 miles." Shorty did not answer. Instead, he mounted his horse and rode away, whistling and shaking his head in a digusted manner. This made Pete angry and he chased after him yelling as he ran. An angry Basque is something not to trifle with, so Shorty pulled up and waited.

When Pete came up, he said, "Come on, Pete, let's get on to Ballarat." "Not until you have looked at this rock," Pete replied. He was still hot under the collar. Grudingly, Shorty took out his magnifying glass and squinted at the rock. Jumping from his horse, he cried, "Holy Smokes! Fourth of July! We're rich! Where in the hell did you find this Pete!" The gold strike had been made, not by Shorty Harris, but by Pete Aguereberry. However, Shorty told people he made the strike. When asked where Pete fit in on the discovery, his answer was, "Ah! he's just a Frenchman who was traveling with me when I made the strike."

This writer's version of what happened after the strike was made, will differ from what has been written before in books published on Death Valley. Other authors have touched lightly on the discovery of gold at Harrisburg. Some gave Shorty the credit for the strike, while others gave it to Pete. No author spent as much time with Pete Aguereberry as I did. I visited him at different intervals for days at a time. Many a night we sat by the wood stove in his immaculate cabin and talked until the sun was peeping over Aguereberry Point.

It is not my intention to belittle Frank "Shorty" Harris, nor is it my intention to glorify Pete Aguereberry. They both have passed to the great beyond. They were rugged individuals, trail blazers, desert men, Death Valley men. Men of a hardy race who pioneered the Death Valley country.

There are two sides to every controversy. The writer knew Shorty Harris, but not as well as he knew Pete Aguereberry. Pete disliked Shorty, and he was undoubtedly biased in his side of the story. The writer never got Shorty's version of the strike and what happened afterward. But, after knowing Shorty and having talked with other oldtimers who knew both men well, we would have to go along with Pete's story.

When Pete overtook Shorty in Wood Canyon and showed him the gold-bearing rock, Shorty immediately lost all interest in celebrating the Fourth of July in Ballarat. Shorty said, "It's better than Bullfrog, Pete. They cheated me out of Bullfrog. All I ever got out of Bullfrog was $700, but they are not going to cheat me out of this." Shorty was all for going back and staking the whole hill, but Pete talked him out of it, telling him that he was short of grub, and it was best they go on to Ballarat and replenish their supplies and then return to the site of the strike. Shorty said, "Hell! Pete,we're partners now. I've got plenty of grub and I'll divide with you." Pete replied, "That's fine, but we're short of water and we will have to go on to the nearest spring and replenish our supply." "Okay, we'll go down to Wildrose Spring, camp for the night and return tomorrow," said Shorty. Pete had Shorty's pledge that if they met anyone on the trail or at the spring, he wouldn't mention the gold strike to them.

By necessity, Wildrose Spring in Wildrose Canyon was a popular camping site and meeting place for prospectors and desert travelers. When Pete and Shorty reached the spring, darkness had fallen. A fellow by the name of Terry (Terry is buried in the Ballarat boothill) and Frank Kennedy, a squaw man, were camped there. Kennedy greeted them saying, "Hi Shorty, what's new?" Shorty replied, "When you see the short man, there's a boom in the making. Meet my new partner, French Pete." Kennedy, knowing Shorty, ignored the statement and shaking hands with Pete, he introduced him to Terry and offered him a drink. Pete felt like batting Shorty over the head with something. Here he was, talking about a boom after promising not to mention it and he didn't even know the exact location of the strike.

Pete and Shorty cooked their supper over the campfire. After relaxing over a couple of smokes, Pete called Shorty aside and suggested they turn in for the night so they could get an early start back to the strike in the morning. Shorty said, "There's no hurry." "Somebody might find it," said Pete. "Hell no," Shorty replied, "People have been jackassin' past that hill for years without seeing it." Pete was dead tired, so he spread his blankets on the ground within hearing distance and retired for the night. Shorty went back to the campfire and the company of Terry and Kennedy. He wasn't about to retire as long as there was conversation and a bottle being passed around. Pete lay and listened as he was afraid to go to sleep for fear Shorty's tongue would loosen up to the point where he would tell about the strike.

Frank Kennedy later became the county recorder for the Wildrose Mining District. Through his willingness to help his fellow man, he had a lot of friends. Later, he and Pete were to go for their guns over a claim jumping incident.

Kennedy had several special-made 10-gallon water cans. They were so constructed that two of them could be packed on a burro at a time. Shorty borrowed ten of the cans from Kennedy. Early the next morning when they left Wildrose Spring they were packing over 100 gallons of water. It would take a lot of water for themselves, the burros and gold panning. Panning was the prospectors way of assaying the value of his find on the spot.

Pete's and Shorty's spirits were high that bright July morning as their burro train wound up colorful Nemo Canyon. They had found gold and now they were returning to do some panning and stake claims for their grubstaking partners. Shorty had so many grubstaking partners that when he found anything worthwhile, usually he had little left for himself when he got through dividing it up. As they rode along in the warm sun-drenched canyon they fell to discussing what to name the new strike site. Pete suggested calling it "Aguereburg." Shorty, never one to be shoved out of the limelight, thought awhile and then came up with "Harrisberry." To this Pete agreed, for after all Shorty was well known in Death Valley country and his name might help the sale of the claims.

When they reached the gold hill they pitched camp and turned the burros loose to feed. Taking their prospecting picks, gold pans and a can of water each, they climbed to the ledge on the north side of the hill where Pete had made the original discovery. Pete told Shorty to pan the ledge on the south side of the hill and he would pan the north side. Crushing and panning some rock, a lot of gold dust showed up in the pan. The sight of gold excited him and he yelled for Shorty. Shorty would not answer. Three times he yelled and still Shorty wouldn't answer. The fourth time he yelled that he had found the right spot, Shorty answered and came scrambling over the hilltop.

When Pete showed him the gold in the pan, he crushed some rock and made a panning. He panned three times and each time the panning was better. Highly elated, he exclaimed, "Fourth of July, Pete, more ham and eggs." "Let's pan the big ledge and if it shows up as good as this we've got the world by the tail on a downhill drag." But when they panned the big ledge there was no color. Shorty, easily discouraged said, "To hell with this claim, I'll sell for $1,000." "Sell what? You haven't got a claim yet," Pete answered. Pete told him that as the ledge went down the gold would probably show up again and asked him if he wanted to stake 1,500 feet on the south side of the hill and he would stake the same on the north side. "Whatever you say," was Shorty's reply. All the next day Pete prospected the hill to the north and Shorty prospected to the south. The following day Pete worked south and Shorty worked north. Pete found some good rock and panned several ounces of gold dust, which he did not tell Shorty about.

Their burros had strayed in the direction of Emigrant Spring toward Death Valley. Shorty said that he would go after them for they might take a notion to go back to Bullfrog. Pete said, "Hell, Shorty, you know them burros are too smart to cross Death Valley in the summer heat." "Oh yes, they might, for they know there's good barley to be had at Bullfrog," was Shorty's reply. Pete tried to talk him out of going after the burros, fearing that he would meet someone at the spring and tell them about the strike. Shorty went anyway. While he was gone, Pete staked four more claims for himself, naming them the Eureka 1, 2, 3 and 4 and put up the monuments. He also staked four claims for Shorty on the other side of the hill. Shorty could write after a fashion, about as well as a third grader in school. Pete had made out three location notices and was working on the fourth when the tinkling of the burro bells heralded Shorty's return.

When Shorty rode up, Pete told him that he had staked four more claims for him and made out the location notices and that he would have to sign them. Shorty said, "To hell with this hill, it's nothing but lime, schist and shale (a favorite expression of Shorty's). I'm going to Ballarat where there's drinks to be had and gold to be found in the mountains nearby. I know where the gold is and someone else does too, but I am going to beat 'em to it." Pete was dumbfounded at this. There were times when Shorty talked and acted like a nut and this was one of the times. It suddenly dawned on him that Shorty was trying to discourage him off the hill for some reason. He patted the gold dust in his money belt and was glad that he hadn't told Shorty about it. Pete knew what Shorty had said wasn't true. He knew that all Shorty wanted was an excuse to go to Ballarat, where he could hoist his foot on a brass rail and tell everyone who set up the drinks about the great gold strike the short man had made at Harrisberry.

Pete picked up his tools and started up the hill. He had climbed a short distance when he heard a banging of the water cans. Hurriedly retracing his steps he found that Shorty had unscrewed the caps of the remaining water and kicked the cans over. Pete became angry, so angry that he started to strike Shorty. Controlling his temper, he cooled off. He had intended staying a while longer to finish the claim staking, but now without water and grub the decision to leave was made, he certainly was not going to eat any more of Shorty's grub. He packed his burros and pulled out ahead of Shorty. One of his burros had taken a liking to one of Shorty's burros and a few miles down the canyon the burro turned back. Pete went after it and met Shorty on the trail. Traveling together, by the time they reached Wildrose Spring, they had patched up their differences, so Pete thought.

Shorty reached the spring first. Kennedy and Terry were still camped there. Pete rode up in time to hear the following conversation. Shorty was talking, "I tell you the short man has something this time, bigger and better than Bullfrog." Then he began showing the specimen. Pete stood outside the light of the campfire, outraged and helpless. "There'll be a thousand men in Harrisburg in a month, thousands in a year," Shorty told them. "I thought we agreed to call it Harrisberry," Pete exclaimed as he stepped in to the light of the campfire. "Fourth of July, Pete, it's going to be the biggest camp in this part of the country," was Shorty's sly way of avoiding Pete's question.

Next morning Pete's saddle burro was gone. Shorty promised to wait at the spring while Pete searched for the burro. Returning that night without having found the burro, dog tired and hungry, he found that Shorty had departed for Ballarat leaving him without any grub. Kennedy and Terry shared grub with him. For two days he hunted the burro without luck. He had become greatly attached to the burro since it had saved his life in Death Valley, and too, it was a fine animal. He had been offered $75 for the burro.

At night wild horses came to the spring. On the morning of the third day he identified a small track mingled with theirs as that of his burro. He followed the tracks to Big Flat near Pinto Peak, a distance of 10 miles from Wildrose Spring, before finding his burro and the horses. He couldn't catch the burro, so he tried driving the herd toward Wildrose Canyon, but they went up Wood Canyon. Twice they doubled back to Pinto Peak. It was July, and hot even in the mountains. He was without water and had run so much that he was about pooped. Finally, heading them off by shooting in front of them, he got them started in the direction of Wildrose but they went down Nemo Canyon. At sundown, exhausted and thirsty, Pete gave up the chase. He was only a mile from Wildrose Spring but he was so all-in that he could only go a hundred yards between rests. When he finally reached the spring no one was there. Kennedy and Terry were out prospecting. He drank six or seven tomato cans of water and was still thirsty. He would have drank more, but he began to retch violently; everything turned black and he had a chill. Darkness had fallen when Kennedy and Terry rode in. They found Pete in a bad way. Wise in the ways of the desert they moistened his lips and gave him sips of water at slow intervals.

The next afternoon some Indians rode in on horses. They had finished haying at Greenland Ranch and had come to the Panamints to spend the rest of the summer. Among them was Joe Kennedy who was Frank Kennedy's half-breed son and Enacio Joaquin, another half-breed. Frank Kennedy had them ride out and catch Pete's burro. It was dark when they returned. Pete was so anxious to reach Ballarat and see what Shorty was up to, that he packed his burros and pulled out. Before leaving, Kennedy gave him a little flour and a small piece of bacon. Pete rode out of the canyon and south to the mouth of Tuber Canyon where he camped for the remainder of the night. Up at the crack of dawn, he made a little weak coffee, fried the small piece of bacon and had flour enough for three flapjacks. He drank the coffee, ate the bacon and one flapjack. The two remaining flapjacks were carefully wrapped and stowed in the chuck box. That was all the food he had and it would have to last until he got to Ballarat.

At Warm Springs, seven miles north of Ballarat, he stopped to water his burros. Warm Springs (known today as the Old

Indian Ranch) was the home of Indian George Hansen and his family. Indian George was famed for two things: longevity and having seen the gold rush emigrants in Death Valley and the Panamint Mountains in the winter of 1849-50. No one really ever knew the exact age of an early Indian as no vital statistics were kept. But according to Jim Boyles, old-time Trona butcher and longtime friend and unofficial agent for the Panamint Indians, George was born at Surveyor Well in Death Valley about the year 1841. If so, he would have been around 63 years old when Pete watered his burros at Warm Springs. George could have been 102 or 103 when he died September 18, 1943. He is buried somewhere in the giant mesquites north of Warm Springs in Panamint Valley.

George's age was calculated from the story he told about the emigrants he saw when he was a little boy. He held his hand about four feet above the ground. (Maybe eight or nine years old). He said, "The snow was on See-umba (Telescope Peak) when a strange tribe of other people (the Jayhawker and the Manly-Bennett Party, 1849) came down Furnace Creek Wash, some walking slow like sick people and some in big wagons pulled by cows. They stopped there by Furnace Creek water and rested. When other Indians see them, they run away and tell all other Indians at other camps.

"Our people were afraid of these strange people and these cows they had never seen before. Never had they seen wagons or wheels or any of the things these people had. The cows were spotted and bigger than the biggest mountain sheep, with long tails and big horns. They moved slow and cried in a long voice like they were sick for grass and water.

"Some of the people moved down the valley, and some moved up, and they stopped at Salt Creek crossing. Them that moved down the valley stopped where Indian Tom Wilson had ranch at Bennett's Well. When it come night we crawl, close, slow-like when trailing sheep. We saw many men around a big fire. They killed cows and burned the wagons and made a big council talk in loud voices like squaws when mad. Some fall down sick when they eat skinny cows. By and by they went away, up that way (where Stove Pipe Wells Hotel is now), they walk very slow, strung out like sheep, some men help other men that are sick. One man, he go no more, he lay down by big rock. That night he went to his father.

"As they go, they drop things all along the trail, maybe they are worthless things, or too heavy to carry. After they go we went to that place at Salt Creek and find many things that they left there. Because one died, we did not touch his things. When they burned the wagons some parts did not burn that were iron, and we did not understand this.

"Those people who went down the valley to Bennett's Well, stayed there a long time. They had women and children (the Manly-Bennett party). By and by they went away, all go over Panamints and we never see them again. The hearts of our people were heavy for these strange people, but we were afraid. They had things that made fire with a loud noise (guns) and we had never seen these before. After this happened we were afraid more of the strange ones would come. We watched Furnace Creek for a long time but no more come.

"Maybe about three or four summers after this, I was on the trail with my father in Emigrant Canyon, when we see man tracks that were not made with moccasins. My father, he say, 'Look, not made by Shoshone.' We follow these tracks and when we come around by big rock we see a white man very close. When we see him we stop quick, I run away. That's how I got my Indian name, Bah-vanda-sava-nu-kee (boy who runs away). This white man made peace sign to my father and give him a shirt. When I see this, I come back. That place was near Emigrant Spring."

The Death Valley and Panamint Indians (Shoshone) were the most southerly of the Shoshonean tribe whose nation stretched as far north as Montana.

Down through the years Pete and the Warm Springs Indians were on friendly terms . . . especially Molly, George's granddaughter, who herded their band of angora goats. They had something in common, as Pete had been a sheepherder.

CHAPTER X

BALLARAT

When Pete punched his burros into Ballarat that hot July afternoon, he was entering for the first time a wild boom town that had already reached its peak and was on the decline, but not so that he could notice. The town had derived its name from the famous mining town of Ballarat in Australia. It was situated on the floor of Panamint Valley, nestled against the base of the Panamint Mountains, near the mouth of Pleasant Canyon. It was a supply center for the mines in the Panamint, Argus and Slate Range Mountains. It was also the terminal of the Johannesburg and Darwin stage and freight lines. Ballarat was founded shortly after gold was discovered up in Pleasant Canyon in 1895. The greatest boom days were from 1897 to 1900. However, it held on as an active town until the end of World War I. There was a post office there from 1897 to 1917. During its short twenty-four year span of life even after the first big boom, the town was rejuvenated on a small scale a few times when a new strike would be made in the area. At one time during its life, there were four gold mills working in the nearby mountains at the following mines: The Ratcliff was the largest, with a twenty stamp mill; the O Be Joyful, with ten stamps; the Anthony, with five; and the Cooper, with four. These mines produced more than a million dollars in gold.

When Pete arrived, the town boasted a population of 500, actually 250 would have been nearer right as it was a floating population. When it was payday at the mines, sometimes the population more than doubled when the miners came to town for a spree.

There were several saloons of which Chris Wicht's emporium of drink and pool parlor was the most popular place in town. The pool table had been brought around Cape Horn to San Francisco in 1875, and freighted up to Panamint City. When Panamint City became a ghost town, Chris acquired the pool table. He had made a fair-sized stake out of the Lila C. Borate Mine, on the Amargosa side of Death Valley, which financed his entry into the saloon business. He was a showman, for on the hottest days of summer— and its gets hot in Ballarat—he would take his turn at bartending, attired in a long swallow-tailed coat, celluloid collar and derby hat. (Chris drank himself to death at the age of 80. He died on October 17, 1944 and is buried in Argus, California.)

Among the lesser establishments of the town was the stage depot, a couple of general stores and a hotel. There was also a boot-hill, which would be listed today as the only remaining permanent establishment. There was also an assay office presided over by Fred Gray who spent forty-five years in Ballarat.

Judge Richard Decker, who never scratched a pen on his books, assisted by Constable Henry Pietsch, who was also the village blacksmith, kept law and order. That is, until a slight difference of opinion between the agents of the law resulted in the Judge being unchivalrously shot in the back by Constable Pietsch. The Judge crawled out of his office along the wooden sidewalk that bordered the main street of Ballarat before collapsing. The Judge's path along the walk was marked by blood stains. The stains were a source of attraction for many years for the tourists. Dr. Homer R. Evans, Trona's first doctor, recalled having seen the stains as late as 1916. The stains remained until some enterprising soul in need of firewood tore up the sidewalk. When the Judge received the fatal wound, the nearest doctor was at Randsburg, a distance of 65 miles. Ralph Williams, a husky part-time miner and teamster, mounted a big stout mule and rode for the doctor. When he reached Randsburg in record time, the mule dropped dead at the hitching rail. Williams had ridden the mule to death. Dr. Reginald E. MacDonald climbed into his buckboard pulled by four fast horses and headed for Ballarat. The Judge expired at the end of 24 hours. The doctor arrived one hour too late.

The hotel in Ballarat was quite an oddity. It was built in 1898 by Jim Calloway. All the lumber and building material for the hotel was hauled by team and wagon from Johannesburg, which was a branch line terminal of the Santa Fe Railroad. The building had two stories. The ground floor, constructed of adobe, housed the saloon, lobby, dining room and kitchen. The upper floor, built of lumber, contained twelve rooms, which were accessible from a veranda which ran the length and breadth of the building and was reached by an outside staircase. Room rates were only fifty cents a day per person and the price was never raised according to the old-timers.

Among a few of the prominent citizens of the town at the time, not mentioned before, were: Mr. and Mrs. Clair Tyler, Lester Calloway, Jack Calloway, Jack Sweet, Jack Cress, Al Meyers, E. C. York, John Caricart, Domino Etcharren (a Basque who owned and operated a saloon, slaughter house and butcher shop) and Joe L. Foisie who had the distinction of being the only man in Ballarat whose "schnozzle" (nose) was bigger than Chris Wicht's.

Foisie liked to talk about the big poker games in Ballarat. His favorite was about a game in Chris Wicht's saloon in which he sat with Al Meyers, Shorty Borden and Chris. The game was draw poker and the "payoff" hand came just as the stage was leaving for Johannesburg. Foisie had a full house, Meyers a heart flush, Chris threw in his hand and Shorty held four sevens. The betting and raising went on until the three players had all their money in the pot. Came the showdown and Shorty Borden's four sevens won the pot. Scooping up the money he ran out and boarded the stage on his way to San Francisco. Foisie and Meyers never forgave Borden for riding out on them without giving them a chance to recoup their losses.

From a booming mining supply center, Ballarat became a crumbling ghost town as the elements and the vandals took their toll. The population dwindled to one man, the last inhabitant, "Seldom Seen Slim", who lived in a trailer at the end of Main Street. Slim died in August, 1968, and is buried in the Ballarat boot hill. Four hundred people, including an NBC television crew, braved the August heat to attend the funeral. The following day the funeral was seen on national television.

In 1966 Neil Cummins bought the eighty-acre townsite from Laura May Wagner. He drilled a well, built a small store and trailer park, with the hopes of restoring the old ghost town. That dream was also to fade.

Pete made camp in a roofless adobe across the street from York's general store. When he went to the post office to get the money order from his grubstaking partners, it hadn't arrived. This put him squarely behind the eight ball as he was flat broke (except for the gold dust in his money belt, which he dared not expose), out of grub and hungry. On the way back to camp he entered York's store, where he eyed the great piles of flour, beans, lard, potatoes, slabs of bacon and the other edibles. Being too proud to beg, borrow, or ask for credit, he walked out of the store, hoping that tomorrow's mail would bring the money order. Shorty Harris was in town fairly well "liquored up" but Pete steered clear of him.

Mr. York had a long telescope and when the daily stage from Johannesburg was about due to top the Slate Range Crossing, he would stand in the middle of the street and eye the summit through the telescope. When the stage appeared on the skyline, he would enter Chris Wicht's saloon and he and the boys would make bets on the exact time of the stage's arrival in Ballarat.

Pete was killing time in Chris' saloon when one of the patrons became boisterous and insulting. Chris, never one to tolerate this, grabbed the fellow by the collar and the seat of the pants and gave him the old "heave ho" out into the dust of the street. Getting up and dusting himself off, the man told Chris that he was going to his cabin after his gun and when he came back he would kill him. Chris got his 30-30 rifle and took a seat with his back to the wall on the front porch of the saloon, waiting the return of the badman. After waiting a reasonable length of time, Chris gave up the vigil and went back into the saloon. A fellow said, "Let me see your rifle," Chris handed it to him and looked on as the fellow discovered that the rifle wasn't loaded.

Ballarat's social life centered in the saloons. There were courtesy beds in the backroom for the benefit of the patrons who drank unwisely . . . which brings to mind our favorite story about Chris Wicht's saloon.

When the mining town of Darwin was booming, Lonnie Lee was a prosperous and respected merchant in the town. When his wife died, he couldn't stand the grief and he went to pieces. He drank himself out of business and out of town, winding up in Ballarat, as a barfly (today they are called winos). In those days when a saloon patron imbided too freely, he wasn't bodily thrown out, or the law called to take him away, he was put to bed in the back room. Every saloon in town had a couple of courtesy beds. This was considered good business, for when the patron sobered up he was a potential customer.

Lonnie would make the rounds of the saloons mootching drinks and, at a late hour, he would become overly tanked and take advantage of a courtesy bed.

There was a clan of Irish miners working at the Ratcliff Mine in Pleasant Canyon above Ballarat. One of their brethren was killed in a mine accident. The Irishmen quit work and took the body down to Ballarat. There was no morgue so they placed the corpse on a courtesy bed in the back room of Chris Wicht's saloon and covered it with a bright colored quilt. While awaiting the arrival of the coroner, who had to travel seventy-five miles by horse and buggy from Lone Pine, the Irishmen proceeded to hold the wake. During the course of the night many drinks were lifted in toast to the departed Mike.

At a late hour, Lonnie, who had been working the other end of town and not knowing about the wake, staggered through the back door seeking a courtesy bed. Seeing the bright quilt, he thought (that is, if he was still able to think) that the quilt covered another drunk, so he crawled under the quilt with the corpse.

Along toward morning he awoke in time to hear an Irishman in the bar bellow, "Set 'um up for the house." Lonnie, cold and with the shakes, wrapped the quilt around his head and shoulders, walked into the bar and announced that he would like a drink too.

The bewildered, drunk and frightened Irishmen thought the corpse had come alive. Along with the bartender they stampeded through the front door splintering it as they went, leaving poor Lonnie and the corpse in sole possession of the saloon.

CHAPTER XI

HARRISBURG GOLD RUSH

Pete had been camped in Ballarat across the street from the general store for two days. He had not built a fire for he had nothing to cook. Mr. York, the storekeeper, not noticing any smoke at Pete's camp sent his clerk, Tom Connell, over to tell Pete he wanted to see him. Mr. York, a devout Catholic, asked Pete if he was French and a Catholic. Pete told him he was. York wanted to know if he intended to spend the rest of the summer in and around Ballarat. Pete told him "no" and explained that he was just a prospector who had come to Ballarat expecting to pick up a money order at the post office, but that it hadn't arrived. He did not mention the gold strike he had made. He told him that when the money order came, he was going to outfit himself with grub and continue prospecting. York asked him how long it had been since he had eaten. Two days, Pete told him. York handed him a dollar and told him to go to the dining room at the hotel and get a square meal and when he came back, he would give him a grubstake.

Reluctantly, Pete accepted the dollar, pangs of hunger had overcome his pride. Thanking Mr. York, he departed for the dining room and for the dollar he ate two meals. At sundown, when he returned, the store was crowded and he politely stood in the background awaiting his turn. As he waited the crowd continued to grow.

It seemed that all the prospectors and miners in town were outfitting to take off to the scene of a new strike. Pete's ears perked up when he got the drift of their conversation which went like this: "Did you hear that Shorty Harris made a new strike?" "Ah! don't believe Shorty. To hear him talk he is always making a new strike." "I don't believe it myself, but he's flopping around like a chicken with its head off, all excited, telling about the rich gold bearing rock he found between Blackwater Canyon and Wildrose Spring at a place he calls Harrisburg." "Says there was a Frenchman with him when he made the strike but the Frenchman hasn't shown up yet."

One fellow said that he was going to round up his burros and pull out early the next morning. Another said that his burros were down by the slaughter house and he was going down and tie them up so that he could leave the next morning. Soon all the fellows in the store joined the chorus, saying that they were going.

Pete had heard enough and he crowded up to the counter. Mr. York, seeing him, came over and said, "Well, Pete what can I do for you?" "I'll take that grubstake now if you will trust me," he answered.

"Trust you," York said, "Why! I've never lost a dime yet, grubstaking a prospector. It's those fly-by-night mining promoters from Los Angeles that I don't trust. You can have all the grub you need and if you strike anything good, stake a couple of claims for me."

York loaded Pete up with $19.00 worth of grub, which was a lot in those days. Bacon sold for 19¢ a pound, potatoes 1½¢ per pound and other commodities were as cheap accordingly.

Pete was not going to wait until morning to depart. Lugging the supplies out of the store and hurriedly packing them on the burros, he headed into the night for Harrisberry, which Shorty had renamed Harrisburg. By riding hard he reached Wildrose by noon. He knew that he was ahead of the horde of gold seekers from Ballarat and he wanted to stay ahead of them, but he was so tired that he was forced to stop at the spring to eat and sleep for a few hours. Late afternoon found him again on the trail. He had pulled out just as the vanguard from Ballarat was arriving at the spring.

The hills of Harrisburg were bathed in moonlight when he rode up to his claim at 2:00 a.m. There was no sign of life on the hill and with a sigh of relief he started unpacking his burros. He was busily engaged with the work, when the burros went on the alert, with ears pointed forward they were looking upward. Pete looked up and saw a lone figure silhouetted by the moonlight on the crown of the hill. The figure was slowly working its way in and around the rocks down the hill toward him. Pete's hand wrapped around the butt of his gun as he stood motionless in the shadow of the burro. As the figure drew near he saw that it was a man, at first he thought that it was Shorty Harris, but when he saw the man was larger than Shorty he wondered who it was.

As the man drew near, in a gruff voice he asked, "What in the hell are you doing here?"

"The same to you brother. What the hell you doing here?" Pete answered.

"Who told you there was a strike here?" the man asked.

In a surprised tone of voice Pete answered, "Is there a strike here?"

"Yes, Shorty Harris made a strike here and has located the south side of the hill and I have located the north side," the man said.

"North side! Where?" Pete asked as his blood began to boil.

The fellow answered, "See that monument over there. That's one of my corners."

"Your corner and your monument? Hell, I built that monument there myself," Pete told him.

"You built it? Why, you couldn't have built it. There wasn't anyone here ahead of Shorty," the man exclaimed.

"The hell there wasn't. I'm the man who made the strike here," Pete yelled back.

As the argument grew louder, Pete's grip on the butt of his gun grew tighter. The wise old burros, as they stood patiently in the moonlight waiting to be relieved of their loads, were the only witnesses to the drama being enacted here high in the Panamint Mountains. The actors, two strangers, with gold fever in their blood, were rapidly reaching the point of no return. The patient burros must have wondered just what constituted a jackass.

Pete said, "Mr., I don't know your name."

"My name is R.M. Thurman," the man cut in.

"My name is Jean Pierre Aguereberry. They call me 'French Pete' and if you will come with me, I'll prove these are my claims."

Thurman followed and watched as Pete dug into the monuments. Pete's location notices were gone, replaced by Thurman's. By the light of a match he saw the notices were signed by Thurman as the locater and witnessed by Frank "Shorty" Harris. Pete smelled a rat. Something was radically wrong—so wrong that he began to realize that he was up against a tough proposition and that he had better cool off and in a sane way try to get to the bottom of it.

Politely he said, "Mr. Thurman, whatever Shorty Harris had here I gave him."

"You gave him?" Thurman snorted.

"Yes, sir. I discovered the gold here and I had to run after Shorty to show him what I had found. I built these monuments and wrote my location notices. Also, trying to be a friend to Shorty, I wrote three of his notices. I can prove this to you if you will let me show you."

"How?" Thurman asked.

By now it was daylight. Pete dug into his pack and got out a blank location notice and a pencil. Writing out the location notice he handed it to Thurman and said, "Let's go over and dig a location notice out of one of Shorty's monuments and I'll let you be the judge as to whether I'm telling you the truth or not." Thurman consented.

They went over the hill to one of Shorty's monuments and Pete dug out the notice. Thurman compared the handwriting and then extended his hand. "My apologies Pete, I felt all along there was something fishy about this." Pete asked if he cared to tell him about it. Thurman told him that he was in Ballarat when Shorty arrived broke and thirsty. Shorty approached him, telling him about the strike he had made and that if he would advance him a certain amount of money he would guide him to the strike and he could stake some good claims. He and Shorty had slipped out of Ballarat a day ahead of Pete. Avoiding Wildrose Spring for fear they would encounter someone who knew them, they went up Nemo Canyon. Shorty, riding his horse, reached the strike site ahead of Thurman and had time to destroy Pete's location notices before Thurman rode up on his burro. Shorty told him that he had built the monuments. When Thurman tore up his location notices, Pete knew he had found a friend who was a square shooter.

Later he learned that Thurman had once been an agent for a steamship line in the Hawaiian Islands. Thurman told Pete to go ahead and write out new location notices and he would sign as a witness. When this was done, Pete asked Thurman if he would witness three more claims that he wanted to locate in Mr. York's name, to which Thurman agreed. Mr. York had only asked Pete for two claims but Pete felt so kindly toward him for the grub-staked that he staked three claims for him. Later York sold the claims for $3,500. Thurman advised Pete to recheck the measurements of his claims, which he did by stepping off three feet at a time, a prospector's practical scale. He was grateful for Thurman's thoughtfulness, for after checking he found that he had shorted himself by several feet. He piled brush on the spots where he would later transfer his monuments.

This was a mistake on his part, but he had to go to Emigrant Spring for water before he could do the work. While making preparations to go, working with the burros, he wondered where Shorty Harris was. He asked Thurman if he knew and was told that Shorty had collected more samples and pulled out for Rhyo-lite a few hours before Pete arrived. Pete, in his mind, recalled that only a few days ago he had made the strike and had cut Shorty in on it. He also recalled that he had suggested to Shorty that after building their monuments and having the claims recorded, they would keep quiet about the strike and, when the weather cooled off in the fall, they would pack their best samples across Death Valley to Goldfield and have them assayed so they would know how rich their claims were and then try to sell them for big money. This was good advice, but not for Shorty. He couldn't get out fast enough to tell about the strike.

Later Pete learned that what little interest Shorty had left in his claims after his grubstakers took their cut, he sold for a thousand dollars of which he was paid seven hundred and given three thousand shares of stock in the hastily formed mining company that bought the claims. Shorty went on a seven-hundred-dollar bender in Goldfield that lasted two weeks. Later, when the mining company slapped a ten-cent a share assessment on the stock, Shorty wasn't able to meet the assessment and he lost the stock. Pete shared his Eureka claims with his original grubstakers, Flynn and Kavanagh, each partner owning a third interest in the claims. Pete held onto his share of the valuable mining property through many troubled years, with the tenacity of a leech, battling tough claim jumpers and crooked mining promoters who hired gunmen to kill him. Not by choice but by necessity, Pete became a tough hombre. He not only won the battles, he won the whole hill as well. In the end he owned all the property.

Pete was aware that he was inviting trouble, big trouble, by leaving the claims unprotected while he was gone to Emigrant Spring for water. But the welfare of his faithful burros came first, and they needed water. He knew that while he was away, the gold-seekers from Ballarat would swarm over the hill like a plague of locusts and in the end, only the strongest would survive. The weaklings would be bluffed or shot out of their legitimate holdings.

Upon his return from Emigrant Spring, he found the hill swarming with men. Men with guns strapped to their hips, all mad with the lust for gold. When he rode up to his claims he found a man building a monument on the spot where he had piled the brush. When the man looked up he saw that it was Frank Kennedy, the squaw man who had befriended him at Wildrose Spring when he ordered the Indians to ride out and find his saddle burro.

Pete asked him what he was doing. Kennedy told him he was building a monument. "My friend, you are building the monument on my claim," Pete told him.

"How come?" was Kennedy's reply.

Pete tried to explain the mistake he had made in measuring the claims. But the explanation did not register with Kennedy, who was in no mood to listen.

Kennedy exclaimed, "What do you want, the whole hill?" "We gave you those claims over there, what more do you want?"

"Nobody gave me any claims. I'm the one who gave the claims away. I gave Shorty Harris the south side of this hill, which I was not obligated to do, and anyone trying to take my side of the hill will have to leave my bones here first," Pete told him in anger.

"Talking about shooting are you?" Kennedy cried.

Kennedy was wearing a horse feed bag strapped to his shoulder which he used to carry ore samples in. He reached into the bag and pulled out a long-barreled revolver. Kennedy found himself looking down the barrel of a six-shooter. Pete had beat him to the draw. "Drop that gun in the bag before I drill you right between the eyes," Pete told him in a deadly voice. Kennedy, one surprised man, meekly obeyed. Pete shoved his gun back in the holster and

coldly explained to Kennedy how the mistake was made in measuring the claims. He also told him that he was the second man who
had tried to jump his claims and the next claim jumper he caught
he was going to shoot first and, if there was any life left in him, he
would argue with him afterwards.

When the Wildrose Mining District was formed, Kennedy
was appointed Deputy County Recorder for the district and, as
the district stretched from Wildrose Spring to Death Valley, Kennedy, at a dollar a claim made a lot of money.

The Honorable Fred Gray, unofficial mayor of Ballarat, was
a member of the committee who picked out the spot for the
townsite which they rightfully named "Harrisberry". However,
Shorty Harris, in his roadrunning ways (he was also known as
the roadrunner, chaparral bird), had spread the name Harrisburg
throughout the Death Valley country and Harrisburg it became.
It is shown on today's maps as Harrisburg Flat.

By September, there were 500 men at Harrisburg. It was
strictly a tent town, even Sam Adams' saloon and general store
was housed in a large tent. Adams freighted his supplies from
Ballarat. It was said that in the first six months of operation, he
made a neat profit of six thousand dollars on the saloon alone.

Ten days from the time Shorty destroyed Pete's location notices, he came back from Rhyolite bringing fifteen men with him.
Their plans were to do some claim jumping, but the great number
of men they found guarding their claims with guns changed
Shorty's and his goldseekers' minds. Shorty pulled out the next
day without having come near Pete. It was well that he did, for
the next time they met face to face, Pete knocked Shorty down.

Pete did the assessment work on the four original Eureka
claims and sent word to Flynn and Kavanagh in Goldfield to come
over and they would go to Independence, the county seat of Inyo
County, where they would draw up and record the ownership
papers. While awaiting their arrival he prospected the surrounding area and located thirty more claims. He let contracts for the
assessment work on them. These claims were his and would remain
so as long as he kept up the assessment work or until they were
sold. He had fulfilled his obligation to Flynn and Kavanagh by
cutting them in on the four Eureka claims.

CHAPTER XII

SHATTERED DREAMS

When Flynn arrived in Harrisburg in late September, he brought Kavanagh's proxy, as Kavanagh was unable to leave Goldfield. After the deeds were drawn up and recorded, Flynn was all for selling the claims at once to the highest bidder. Pete was agreeable, all he wanted was a modest fortune, so he could go to San Francisco and live like a gentleman. Flynn was to handle the sale of the claims for the three partners. When he started the ball rolling things moved fast. They moved into a maze of litigation that was unbelievable.

Flynn first went to Rhyolite where he contacted Sherwood Aldrich, a big man in Nevada mining circles. Aldrich promised to send a mining engineer out to check the claims and cut some samples. Flynn then went to Los Angeles where he put up at the Hollenbeck Hotel which was the favorite stopping place for the desert mining men and promoters. Here, Flynn met Captain Fleece and his brother "Spec" who were supposed to be big-time mining promoters. The two men were interested in the claims, so Flynn took them out to Harrisburg along with their geologist and engineer. After seeing the claims and taking samples, they returned to Los Angeles. Flynn was a heavy drinker, which may have had some bearing on the deal he made with Captain Fleece and his brother. They promised, and it must have been just a promise as they never went through with the deal, to make a down payment of $15,000, put $35,000 in escrow, build a ten-stamp mill, keep the mine in steady production by working three shifts and pay the three partners a good royalty on the gold that was produced. The joker in the deal was that they wanted and got a third interest in the claims.

Friday was Pete's unlucky day. Most of his accidents happened on Friday. In this instance, Friday the 13th was the big pay-off. This was the day Flynn brought the papers to Harrisburg for Pete to sign, closing the deal. Pete was a trusting soul then, a lamb among a pack of wolves, no match for the unscrupulous promoters who slickered people out of their mining property. But he learned, he learned the hard way. Pete favored a straight cash deal, but at the insistance of partner Flynn he reluctantly signed the papers.

For some reason not clear to Pete, Captain Fleece and his outfit never did put up any money. The deal fell through and it was never clear to him how they acquired a third interest in the claims before welshing on the deal. Anyway, Flynn and Pete hired O.K. Jones, a Los Angeles attorney, to try and get the third interest back. At first, lawyer Jones wanted a third interest in the property for his fee. At this, the partners balked. Lawyer Jones would be paid cash for his service, as they had had enough of this third interest business.

While the lawyer was working at retrieving the third interest, Flynn divided his time between Los Angeles and Harrisburg. Pete also had to make a few trips to Los Angeles, which were expensive. The trip was made by horse stage via Trona to Johannesburg and then by rail via Barstow to Los Angeles. At this time, while lawyer Jones was working on the case, he was also working on the side trying to promote the sale of the claims. He let it be known that he had a prospect who would pay $150,000 for the claims and he kept writing to Pete to meet the prospective buyer at the Harrisburg stop on the Skidoo stage line. Pete met the stage a few times but the prospective buyer never showed up.

In the meanwhile, Aldrich had never sent his engineer to check the claims. Pete, tired of waiting for someone else to promote the sale of the claims, thought he would try his luck, so he went to Rhyolite. Aldrich had two partners, McKenzie and Sutherland, who maintained mining offices in Rhyolite. At first Aldrich showed little interest in Pete's sales talk, but when Pete showed him the letter he had received from lawyer Jones mentioning the $150,000 prospective buyer, he became interested. The next day he sent his mining engineer by team and wagon to Harrisburg to investigate the claims. Pete rode back with him. The engineer spent two days inspecting the claims and taking samples.

He intended to remain longer but when he did some panning, so much gold showed up in the pan that he got excited and left immediately for Rhyolite. Before leaving, he told Pete he would probably hear from Aldrich in eight days.

On the eighth day, Aldrich, McKenzie and another mining man came chugging up from Emigrant Wash in a big $16,000 Locomobile. This was the first automobile to come to Harrisburg, and it would never have made it across the sand dunes in Death Valley without the aid of four stout mules. The Indians were camped at Harrisburg at the time in brush wickiups. Shoshone Johnnie's hunchback mother was sitting cross-legged on the ground keeping an eye on the papooses, when the noise of the approaching automobile was heard. Everybody was looking in the direction of the noise. The old squaw shaded her eyes with her hand and stared at the iron monster when it came into view. Jumping up she gathered all the papooses around her and herded them into the wickiup. The Indian bucks were braver and one of them came over to Pete and asked, "What's the matter here? What's the matter here? Gottem' no horse, no push'em, no pull-'em, run like hell, make big noise, what's the matter here?"

It was late in November, the year was 1906, when Aldrich and his party arrived at Harrisburg to inspect the Eureka claims with the expectation of buying them. Aldrich called Pete over to the car and told him that as the day was about spent, they would go back to Emigrant Spring and camp for the night. Returning early the next morning they spent a day and a half looking the claims over and taking samples. Before leaving, Aldrich told Pete that if the samples assayed as good as the ones his engineer had brought in he would buy the claims, if Pete and his partners could produce a clear title.

Aldrich and his party left at noon in a snow storm. Flynn came that night by stage from Los Angeles, bearing good news. He had learned from attorney Jones that within a few days they would have a clear title to the claims.

The storm lasted two days, blanketing Harrisburg under two feet of snow. Four days later Pete and Flynn received a telegram from Aldrich telling them to come to Rhyolite at once. The telegram had been phoned across Death Valley to Skidoo and then taken to Harrisburg by stage.

Pete and Flynn left for Rhyolite riding burros. Due to the deep snow in the Panamint and Funeral Mountains it took them two days to make the trip. They reached Rhyolite in late afternoon. After having dinner, they went to Aldrich's office where the papers for the transaction were drawn up and signed. Aldrich and his partners were paying $180,000 cash for the claims. Pete, Flynn and Kavanagh would each receive $60,000.

The next day Aldrich and Flynn left by train on the Las Vegas and Tonopah Railroad bound for Los Angeles where they would pick up the clear title from attorney Jones.

December the tenth was the day Pete was to pick up the $60,000 at the First National Bank of Rhyolite. He rose early in high spirits, for this was the day he was going to be repaid for all the hardship he had endured as a burro prospector in the Death Valley country. At last he had reached the end of the rainbow, and would collect his pot of gold. He hated to part with his faithful burros, but he couldn't take them with him as he was going to San Francisco to live the life of a gentleman in the Basque colony. He gave the burros to a friend whom he knew would take good care of them.

Dressed carefully in his best clothes, he was standing at the bar in the "66 Saloon", across the street from the bank. He was buying drinks for the house, for after all, in one hour when the bank opened he would be a rich man.

A messenger boy entered the saloon and asked the bartender if he knew Pete Aguereberry. Pete overheard him and said, "I'm your man. I'm Pete Aguereberry."

"I have a telegram for you," the boy told him.

Pete signed for the telegram. He was feeling so good he gave the boy a two-dollar tip.

Ripping the envelope from the message he read five tragic words: "Fleece blocked sale, letter following." For a moment his heart stood still. He was stunned. As his mind slowly started functioning again he crumpled the telegram and tossed it on the floor. Leaving his drink on the bar untouched, he walked out of the saloon and out of town onto the desert. He wanted to be alone where he could think clearly. That night sleep would not come to him. Rolling and tossing he awaited the coming of day, when he would receive Flynn's letter giving the details of what had happened.

The letter brought information that Captain Fleece, his brother "Spec" and their two partners, Levine and McCall, had served injuction papers on Flynn at the Hollenbeck Hotel, blocking the sale. He also informed Pete that attorney Jones had doublecrossed them inasmuch as he had been in cahoots with Fleece and his partners all along. He told Pete not to worry, that Aldrich had wired his attorney in San Francisco to come down and straighten things out for them and when he did, the sale would go through. He also advised Pete to sit tight and keep close-mouthed.

Pete waited for six days in Rhyolite without hearing any more from Flynn. The time in which they had to do the assessment work on the claims was running short. The work had to be finished by the first of the year, and Pete was the only one to do it.

Sadly, he went to the friend to whom he had given the burros. After explaining what had happened and apologizing for being an Indian-giver, he got the burros back and went back across Death Valley to the bleak snow-covered mountains at Harrisburg. It was the longest trip he ever made. At least it seemed to be the longest.

Christmas day found Pete and a crew of men he had hired toiling away doing the assessment work on the claims. A far cry from the plans he had made to spend Christmas day in the gay city of San Francisco with his brother Arnaud.

A month later Flynn, on his way to his home in Nevada, stopped at Harrisburg to inform Pete that Captain Fleece and his partners had the claims so hopelessly tied up in litigation that he doubted if they could ever sell the claims unless they sold them to Captain Fleece and his gang for little or nothing.

The promoters knowing they had them over a barrel had offered to buy their interest at a ridiculously low figure. Flynn told Pete that he and Kavanagh were so burned up and disgusted over the way things had turned out that they would see Captain Fleece and his crowd in hell, before they would sell to them at their price; that he and Kavanagh did not intend to spend any more of their time and money fighting the promoters in court; and that they had reached a decision to relinquish their interest in the claims to him. Deeds would be drawn up to that effect.

When this was done, Pete owned the controlling interest in the claims. He was on his own. One man against a group of smart promoters who were not above using underhanded methods to get rid of him. But, in the end, Pete out-foxed the smart boys and became the sole owner of the claims.

Indian George Hansen, Chief of Panamint tribe, at Warm Springs Ranch during the 1920's.

Rare white burro (with band of angora goats in background) at Panamint Valley's Warm Spring Ranch, when the Indians lived there.

Main Street of Ballarat as it looked in 1917.

Rare photograph of Frank "Shorty" Harris and "Seldom Seen Slim" in Ballarat, circa the 1920's.

Mercantile store on north side of Ballarat's "Main Street".
Porter Brothers were the original owners.

Chris Wicht, Ballarat's best remembered saloon keeper.

Pete Aguereberry's home at the Eureka Mine in Harrisburg Flats, as it was in 1941. Painting in foreground is by Trona artist, Virgil Trotter.

Pictured here at his Eureka Mine is Pete Aguereberry, as he sorts high-grade ore. The compressor building is on the left and the blacksmith shop on the right, background.

This rare photo shows workmen preparing to stop leak in the Skidoo water pipeline in Harrisburg Flats. Time period: the Winter of 1915.

The second hanging of Joe L. "Hootch" Simpson in a tent at Skidoo. The body had been exhumed for benefit of the press.

Indian George Hansen heading north for his Panamint Valley home after shopping at the Trona Company store, circa 1929.

Pete Aguereberry standing on "Aguereberry Point" overlooking Death Valley.

Four stalwart residents of Ballarat: (left to right) "Seldom Seen Slim", Billy Hyder, Fred Grey and Chris Wicht.

—ROBERT A. CARTTER

Pete Aguereberry at his home in November, 1935.

Sam Ball, Death Valley prospector and miner, in Wildrose Canyon, October, 1942.

The "Mexican Central" train at Trona, Calif., about 1918-19; Oscar Johnson is the engineer. Pete rode the train across Searles Lake to Copper Queen Mine during WWI.

Model-T-Ford crossing dry lake in Panamint Valley, about 1916. Camp of Ballarat is barely visible in background.

Pete Aguereberry and nephew Ambroise Aguereberry at the Eureka Mine.

*Spending a quiet Sunday afternoon at Wildrose Station in 1943, are
(left to rt.): Pete Aguereberry, Martin Broshan and Charley Nunn.*

The last picture of Pete Aguereberry, shortly before his death in 1945.

The author and Pete Aguereberry's Ford pickup truck in which we took the wild ride down the mountain. This photo was taken (in 1968) at George Greist's Argenta Mine in Wood Canyon.

CHAPTER XIII

SKIDOO

"SKIDOO"

"Up the hills from Ballarat some forty miles or more,
The man who made the Panamints, he left a ledge of ore;
The man who made the Panamints had something on his mind,
He left the ledge of ore in sight for you and me to find;
It's forty miles from Ballarat, the mountains that are blue,
The place is number twenty-three; they named the spot Skidoo."

In the winter of 1906, Harry Ramsey, whose name stood near the top in Nevada mining history, and One-eyed Thompson were on their way from Rhyolite to booming Harrisburg when they lost their way on top of a cloud-shrouded mountain in the Panamints. While stumbling around in the dense mist, they accidently discovered a rich ledge of gold-bearing quartz. The spot where they made the find was soon to become known as Skidoo.

When they finally reached Harrisburg, the clouds had lifted from the mountain top and so had their interest in Harrisburg. They were confident that they had found something bigger and better than Harrisburg. They were right, for the ore was exceedingly richer and in no time seven hundred people created another boom town. Men at Harrisburg whose claims were not proving out, deserted them and went to the new strike at Skidoo which was only ten miles north of Harrisburg.

The name Skidoo never failed to create comment among those hearing it for the first time. They wondered about the name. It's an amusing story. Bob Montgomery, a prominent and prosperous mining man in Nevada, owned and was operating the famous Montgomery-Shoshone Mine at Rhyolite when the strike was made. Hurrying to the scene he bought twenty-three claims from the original locaters and immediately started development work.

Montgomery's presence as an owner created a lot of interest. He was well known throughout the country as a shrewd investor. There was a legend about him that everything he touched in the mining game turned to gold.

The new mining camp was without water. The nearest water was thirteen miles down the mountain at Emigrant Spring in Emigrant Wash. The water was hauled up the mountain by team and wagon for two dollars a barrel, which was pretty expensive water. So when Bob Montgomery announced that he was going to pipe water into the camp and that there would be ample water for everyone at a nominal cost, his stock went up another 100% in the eyes of the local residents. Montgomery needed water, a lot of water, to operate the big gold mill he was building on the north side of the gulch below his mine.

One day the citizens suddenly became conscious that the new camp had no name. A meeting was called to give it a name. Every person in the new camp attended. The first motion from the floor was to name it "Montgomery" in honor of its most esteemed citizen, "Bob Montgomery." The motion was immediately closed and a vote taken. Everyone present voted "Aye", except one lone person, Bob Montgomery.

Montgomery, in no uncertain terms, declared that no town should ever bear his name. Argument and pleading failed to change his mind, and the chairman had to re-open the motion. A new motion was made and unanimously carried to name the town "Hovic", after another well-known citizen, Steve Hovic. He was just as stubborn as Montgomery about a town bearing his name. This stymied the meeting for a while as no one could seem to think of an appropriate name. Finally, a rough garbed inebriated miner standing in the back of the audience called out: "Mr. Sharman, Mr. Sharman, how about calling her by a real name? Let's call'er Skidoo 23. Yes sir. That's a real name, Skidoo 23."

At that time "23 Skidoo" was a popular bit of slang which meant "scram" or "ok" or something. The drunk had reversed the phrase. Loud laughter of haw-haws greeted the motion, but as everyone was familiar with the saying, the motion was unanimously carried to name the town "23 Skidoo." "23 Skidoo" it was, until the post office department was petitioned. The postal authorities balked at the numerals attached to the name, and in order to obtain the post office the "23" had to be dropped from the name.

Eighteen months later, Montgomery's eight-inch pipeline was completed at a cost of $250,000, and then there was plenty of water for everyone—even enough for bathing. The 23-mile pipeline brought water from Birch Spring located at the head of Jail Canyon on the northwest slope of Telescope Peak. The force of the water flowing from a much higher altitude down to Skidoo (elevation 5,680 feet) created a terrific head pressure in the pipeline. The head pressure at Skidoo was 500 pounds and where the line crossed Harrisburg Flat, the pressure was up to 800 pounds. The force of the high pressure water furnished the power to operate Montgomery's stamp mill.

During World War I, the pipeline was salvaged and sold as scrap iron for $37,000. The money panic of 1907 threatened to put the skids under Skidoo, but she came back strong in 1908 and 1909. The ore was rich while it lasted, some assayed as high as $30,000 a ton. However, the mines were shallow and it did not take the experienced miners long to remove the high grade ore.

Off and on, down through the years, leasers have worked the old mines. Where one was lucky and made a little money, dozens of others failed. I remember at the start of World War II, leasers were working the mines and had a mill running in Emigrant Wash. The government's ban on tool steel and powder stopped all gold mining.

The lynching of Joe "Hootch" Simpson in April, 1908 probably did more than anything else to put Skidoo on the map. This gruesome affair will be later related in the story as Pete witnessed the lynching.

The mining company that bought Shorty Harris' four "Cashier" claims on the south side of the hill at Harrisburg, was headed by Dr. Price who was the president and general manager. When Bob Montgomery completed the pipeline, making water accessible at Harrisburg, Dr. Price's company built a ten stamp mill and went into full scale production. The mine was rich and as the gold poured from the mill the stockholders were handsomely rewarded in dividends.

Meanwhile Pete's four Eureka claims on the north side of the hill lay idle, hopelessly tied up in litigation. Pete had thirty or more claims scattered from the Eureka claims all the way to the summit of the mountain overlooking Death Valley. Some of these claims he sold or leased at a fair price. One claim in particular, "The Napoleon", which he had done quite a bit of development work on, lay a quarter of a mile south of the Eurekas. He leased this claim to a couple of men who in six months time took $35,000 in gold out of the mine and then pulled out, leaving the mine in bad shape. In telling about this, Pete complained about the men ruining the mine, by gopher holing for the high-grade ore and by improperly timbering, causing cave-ins which left the mine full of debris. It was obvious that Pete was a bit envious about the $35,000.

Now that Pete was in the chips he built a snug little cabin near Montgomery's pipeline. He no longer had to ride a burro, so he went to Ash Meadows in Nevada and bought a fine saddle horse from a rancher. He thought nothing of riding thirty to seventy miles or more to Coso, Darwin, Olancha or Rhyolite. When Skidoo was active he made frequent trips there for supplies.

When the news of the gold strike at Skidoo reached Los Angeles, Captain Fleece and his brother wasted no time in coming to Skidoo where they leased a claim and started right in mining. Leaving his brother in charge of operations at the mine, Fleece spent most of his time in his Los Angeles office.

Pete made several trips to Los Angeles to see him, trying to reach some agreement whereby they could start mining operations on the Eureka claims. The trips were expensive and he wasn't getting through to Fleece. Finally on the last trip he called for a show-down. Fleece promptly made him an offer of $10,000 for his interest in the claims. This ridiculously low offer only added insult to injury, inasmuch as Fleece had previously blocked the sale of the claims, knocking Pete out of receiving $60,000 for the third interest he owned at the time. Pete, with strong language, told him what he thought about him and that if he never saw him again it would be too soon.

A few days later when Pete reached Johannesburg enroute to Harrisburg, he came face to face with Fleece and his party who were waiting to take the stage to Ballarat. Fleece greeted Pete, as though nothing had happened between them, with these words:

"Why, hello Pete. Glad to see you. Meet Mr. Smith, our Mining Engineer. We are on our way to Skidoo and are going to stop at Harrisburg and take some samples from our claims." To this Pete made no answer, but he thought, "Like hell you are." Pete tried to give him the cold shoulder, but Fleece didn't seem to mind as he continued to be friendly and jovial.

When the stage was ready to depart for Ballarat, they climbed aboard with several bottles of whiskey, which would help relieve the monotony of the twelve hour journey. Every time a bottle made the rounds it was passed to Pete. Feeling there would be trouble before the journey ended, he would tilt the bottle and pretend that he was drinking. When the stage reached Ballarat all the passengers were high except Pete.

Fleece's chauffeur met them in Ballarat with Fleece's car. After having a meal at the Calloway Hotel and making rounds of the saloons, they piled into the car and invited Pete to ride with them. He did not want to go with them, but knowing that the car would beat the stage to Harrisburg, he climbed in with his mind fully made up that he wasn't going to let them take any samples from the Eureka claims.

The party continued drinking and when they reached the Wildrose Canyon they were hilariously banging away at the canyon walls with their guns. Fleece stuck his gun under Pete's nose and pulled the trigger, burning powder from the explosion stung his face. As Pete's hand slipped around the gun concealed under his coat, he said, "Mister, be careful with that gun." The cold glint in Pete's eyes warned Fleece that he and his cronies had better knock it off—which they did by putting the guns away.

During the course of the journey, Pete overheard Fleece tell engineer Smith that he owned two-thirds interest in the Eureka claims, which was untrue, as Pete was two-thirds owner. When they arrived at Harrisburg, Pete jumped out of the car first, pulled his gun on them and ordered them to drive on to Skidoo. He told Fleece that if he took any samples from the claims, he would have to take them over his dead body. The chauffeur hastily drove away.

Later Pete learned through friends, that Fleece and his brother were airing it around Skidoo that Pete was a stubborn illiterate Frenchman, who wouldn't listen to reason and they intended to run him out of the country. Pete never knew for sure that Fleece and his brother were behind the misfortunes that later befell him, but he strongly suspected they were.

CHAPTER XIV

THE LYNCHING *of* "HOOTCH" SIMPSON

Pete had just returned to Harrisburg from a trip to Owens Valley. He was sick with a cold that almost had him down. He found that his horse was missing and started to search for it. Ed McDonald and Sam Crawford shared a cabin on the south side of the ridge. Crawford owned a saddle horse which he kept in a corral alongside the cabin. He had always been friendly, so Pete went to his cabin with the intention of borrowing the horse, to ride out and look for his horse. When he knocked, McDonald opened the door, Crawford wasn't at home. McDonald invited him in and offered him a chair. He asked McDonald if he had seen his horse. The reply was negative. They were conversing in a congenial manner when the door opened and Crawford entered, with his hand inside the front of a blue wool shirt that he was wearing. Without rising Pete said, "Hello Crawford." He then saw that Crawford was very angry about something. Crawford, in an uncontrollable voice stormed at Pete, "You, you Dago s.o.b., you insult me by entering my cabin."

Astonished, Pete asked, "Why, what's the matter, Crawford? I don't understand."

Crawford pulled a gun from his shirt and in great rage yelled at Pete, "Pull your gun and prepare to die, you Dago s.o.b.!"

Pete jumped to his feet and said, "I'm unarmed. I have no gun, Crawford."

Pete knew that Crawford was going to shoot him and the odds of coming out alive against a man with a gun aimed at him at short range was pretty slim, but he would go down fighting. Quick as a cat he dived at Crawford's knees.

The gun roared as Crawford went down in his grasp. The bullet glanced off Pete's head and, momentarily stunned, he was unable to hold onto Crawford. McDonald, who had been laying on his bunk, lunged at Crawford and wrestled the gun from him before he could fire again. Crawford jumped up and ran out of the cabin and out of sight over the ridge.

Pete, blinded by the blood flowing from the wound in his head, slowly got to his feet. Recovering his senses, his first thought was to get Crawford. Staggering over the hill to his cabin, he got his gun. He had to keep wiping the blood from his eyes so that he could see. By the time he returned from looking for Crawford, his boots were full of blood. Crawford was not in sight, so Pete consented to let McDonald examine the wound.

The bullet had grazed the top of his head, fracturing the skull and had embedded a piece of felt from his hat in the fracture. After McDonald had washed the wound and doused it with turpentine, he bandaged it tightly, which stopped the bleeding. He tried to get Pete to lie down while he saddled Crawford's horse and rode to Skidoo for the doctor, but Pete told him that he felt all right—that if he would ride out and find his horse—he would ride to Skidoo and see the doctor. McDonald caught and saddled his horse. Pete mounted and rode away, not in the direction of Skidoo and the doctor, but rather headed west for Coso Hot Springs some thirty miles away.

Pete did not have much faith in doctors and medicine, but he did have great faith in the healing power of the hot mineral water and hot mud that boiled from the volcanic springs at Coso. At the end of two weeks, the severe headache had disappeared, and by the constant application of mud packs on his head, the piece of felt had been drawn from the crack in his skull. The crack healed in time.

At the end of a month Pete returned to Harrisburg and then went to Skidoo in time to attend Crawford's hearing. Pete refused to testify against Crawford as he wanted to take care of him in his own way, which he did. Crawford was released and when he left the building, Pete was waiting for him and he proceeded to work him over with his fists giving him a severe beating in front of the miners who had attended the hearing. He tried to beat a confession out of him as to why he had tried to kill him, but Crawford wouldn't talk. In fact he wasn't able to talk. There's no question but what the men who inhabited the Panamints in those days were muy tough hombres.

When the money panic of 1907 hit Harrisburg and Skidoo, those with gold in the ground or in their pockets were the least affected. Pete's philosophy was that gold was safer in the ground or in his cabin where he had some hidden, than it was in the banks, so he was not hurt by the depression.

Pete zealously guarded the Eureka claims and kept up the assessment work for three years. When Fleece and his brother discontinued operations at Skidoo and left the country, Pete let the assessment work on the claims lapse. He then made a deal with a friend whom he could trust, to relocate the claims. When this was done he purchased the claims from his friend. Thus he became sole owner of the property and, in so doing, he outsmarted the smart boys. He immediately started driving a tunnel into the hill following the gold vein. He worked the mine off and on for thirty-five years and according to Bureau of Mines records, he took $175,000 in gold from the mine over that period of time.

At first, and when he was in his prime, he industriously worked the mine alone. It was amazing the great amount of work he accomplished. One has to go through the mine to appreciate the magnitude of his effort.

When he tired of mining, he would lock the mine door and for diversion, go out and work for someone else for a while. For some reason, Pete never mastered the art of loafing. He just had to keep busy.

In 1912 Pete had the distinction of driving the last horse-drawn stage from Darwin to Ballarat through Sheppard Canyon. A super-duper cloudburst later took the road out of the canyon and it was never replaced.

It was not by necessity that he had to work for someone else for a living as he was well fixed, thanks to his mine, but he liked the pleasure of mingling with people on the outside. When he had enough of people, he would go back to the quiet of his mine.

In later years he worked in Trona a few times. (This is where the author met him in 1928.) Sometimes, in the fall, he would combine pleasure with labor by helping ranchers in Owens Valley with the cattle roundup in the High Sierra. While in the mountains he would do some hunting and fishing on the side. Occasionally he did road work for the county and he worked in other mines a few times.

Tom McNalty was mining at Harrisburg where he and Pete were friends. Tom owned a saddle horse and occasionally he and Pete would ride to Skidoo together after supplies and for a little diversion they would play cards and partake of a few drinks.

Pete was never an excessive drinker. He could recall of having been drunk but twice in his life and one of the occasions was when he and McNalty were in Skidoo. Pete and Al Gotcher were playing double pedro for the drinks in a saloon. They were drinking boilermakers, double shots of whiskey chased with warm beer. McNalty was sitting in another card game and was also imbibing. The regularity with which Pete trumped Gotcher's cards made him sore and he started an argument which ended when he slugged Pete and then the fight started. It was a typical bar-room brawl. Pulled apart and cooled off by the men in the saloon, they shook hands and resumed the game. In no time they were fighting again. When they were separated, they decided they had had enough fighting for the evening, so they shook hands again and then proceeded to get drunk together. Pete remembered nothing about knocking glasses and a quart of whiskey off the bar.

At a late hour he and McNalty were helped on their horses and headed in the direction of home. Somewhere enroute McNalty fell off his horse and slept the rest of the night on the ground. His horse went to Emigrant Spring. Pete managed to hang on and his horse took him home. He managed to get into bed but when the cabin and the bed started going around and around in opposite directions, he fell onto the cold floor where he spent the rest of the night. That cured Pete, never again did he drink to excess.

It was on a like excursion to Skidoo that he and McNalty witnessed the first lynching of Joe "Hootch" Simpson. Yes, "Old Hootch" was lynched twice. The first time for murder and the second time for the benefit of the press.

Inasmuch as Pete witnessed the lynching of Hootch and inasmuch as the author has Hootch's skull and a man living in Holtville, California has the hanging noose and inasmuch as it is some story, we will tell it in its entirety.

Mrs. Milly Glendenning, wife of a prominent mining man, arose early and gazed out the window of the upstairs apartment where she resided in Skidoo in 1908. She screamed, "My God, what have they done to Hootch?" Young Jimmie, her ten-year-old son sprang out of bed and ran to the window to see what had happened to Hootch. There in the bright April sunshine, his grotesque body hung limply by a rope from a telephone pole across the street. The end had come suddenly to a bad man who three days before had murdered Jim Arnold, a good man whom everyone in Skidoo knew and respected.

The sight of the hanging body was deeply impressed upon the mind of young Jimmie, and when in the summer of the following year, the body of his step-brother, Charles Emory Bodge and a companion, Thomas Flause, were packed out of Death Valley into Skidoo, victims of the deadly summer heat (their bodies had been found beside empty canteens on the floor of the valley), young Jimmie knew that it was a tough land for the just and unjust alike.

Here is the biggest headlined story the *Skidoo News* ever printed:

MURDER IN CAMP
MURDERER LYNCHED with GENERAL APPROVAL
Joe Simpson Shoots Jim Arnold
Dead and is Hanged by Citizens

"The disturbance which has shaken this community to the roots in the past two days, opened on Sunday morning last, when Joe Simpson, familiarly known as Hootch (that being his favorite beverage) held up the Southern California Bank here, for the nimble sum of twenty dollars, that being the sum of his immediate need. He was overpowered before he could collect, and his gun was taken from him. He returned to the bank again (which is located in the store) and became very abusive. Jim Arnold, managing partner in the store, finally put him out. Three hours later, he returned with his gun and deliberately shot Arnold, who was unarmed. He turned and covered the banker, Ralph E. Dobbs, and would probably have killed him had not his attention been diverted. He was overpowered and handcuffed. Arnold died the same evening.

"An inquest on Arnold's body was held on Monday, the jury returned a verdict: Killed by gunshot wound, inflicted by Joe Simpson. Sometime on Wednesday night an armed body of citizens overpowered the sheriff and seized the prisoner and hanged him to a telephone pole. On Thursday, an inquest was held on Simpson's body, the jury finding that he died of strangulation by persons unknown. The body was disposed of.

THE TRAGEDY

"The comparative quiet of Sunday morning was broken by a wild disturbance that resulted in the brutal murder of James Arnold, one of the most prominent citizens of the camp, the father of the camp in fact, inasmuch as he located the townsite, and ended in the lynching of his assailant, Joe Simpson, a local saloonkeeper and gunfighter.

"It will go on record as one of the most remarkable lynchings that has taken place in the United States for many years. Joe Simpson, locally known as 'Hootch' owing to his fondness for the liquor known by that name, had been indulging in his favorite stimulant for some days and was in a highly inflamed state. Joe was out of funds, a condition not calculated to improve his usual bad temper, and to his disordered imagination the only practical way of getting it was to kill a banker. For this purpose he crossed the road from the Gold Seal Saloon, which he owned in partnership with Fred Oakes, and entered the Skidoo Trading Company's store, in which the Southern California Bank is located. He immediately covered the cashier, Ralph E. Dobbs with his gun and demanded twenty dollars under penalty of death. In a moment the place was a blaze of excitement. A wild rush ensued and before he could carry out his threat, he was overpowered by a crew of citizens and disarmed by Dr. R.E. MacDonald and Fred Oakes, his partner. He became so abusive to everyone that Jim Arnold, the manager, eventually put him out of the store by force.

"In the meantime Henry Sellers, the deputy sheriff, was on the scene with handcuffs with the intention of securing him to a telephone pole, there being no jail in camp. However, his partner and friend promised to keep guard over him until the necessary warrant could be sworn out for his arrest. He voluntarily went to bed and was soon asleep. His gun was hidden by Oakes.

"Holding up a bank is no light offense, despite the proverbial wooliness of mining camps, and further, he was still under bond of good behavior from the court at Independence, having shot up a hotel there on his last visit. Dwelling on these things, he armed himself with his gun which he had discovered in the oven of the stove and crossed the street.

"He passed the bank counter and approaching Jim Arnold, asked, 'Have you got anything against me, Jim?' and Arnold answered, 'No, Joe, I've got nothing against you.' 'Yes you have, your end has come, prepare to die,' and with that he raised his gun and shot Arnold below the heart.

"In a moment the camp was in an uproar. As rabbits from a warren, armed men sprang from every direction in every state of clothing, and carrying arms of every size and vintage from the half-toy derringer to the mammoth shotgun that tears a man in two, from the hoary flintlock to the cruel Colt Automatic 41 that cuts the bone like cheese. As they dashed up, they stopped, transfixed by the scene before them.

"Gordon McBain, stupid with liquor, and unarmed in any way, attempted to arrest Joe as he stepped from the store, calling on the others not to shoot. Less than fifty yards away, Dr. MacDonald, kneeling in the dirt, with leveled rifle, again and again called on McBain to stand aside, or take the consequences of the bullet meant for Simpson. From the other corner came the constable, with his six-shooter raised, running like a deer and calling on Simpson, who was moving slowly, crouching behind McBain, to submit.

"With a sudden rush they were in the restaurant, where Sellers felled Simpson with a blow on the head, McBain still blundering between the constable and his prisoner. Simpson made a last effort to wrench his hand free, which still clasped his gun, and the constable, realizing that all would be killed in a minute, slipped his gun barrel into McBain's ear and threatened to blow his brains out. Nor was he a second too soon, for Simpson discharged his last three shots at that moment, one bullet passing within an inch of Seller's stomach. Before the zing of the last bullet had ceased, the constable had Simpson overpowered and his gun taken from him by Ben Epstine.

"Simpson, handcuffed, but jubilant at his cowardly crime and at the hot fight he had put up, was taken to the Club Saloon until a guardhouse could be decided upon.

"The lynching took place on Wednesday night. The body was discovered the next morning, hanging, and Judge Theisse advised of the fact. An inquest was held later in the day. While there was a general feeling of levity outside of the court, the investigation was conducted with due dignity. Outside the court, several references were made that provoked a smile. One bystander remarked that he had been awakened twenty-three times during the night to be told that some persons had hanged Joe Simpson. 'I was surprised every time.' Another suggested that the jury returned a verdict that the deceased 'died by visitation of men.' A third remarked that Joe as a 'true Bohemian' until the last, having at his 'positively last appearance, hung around all night,' as was his custom.

"It is somewhat surprising that such an occurance as a public hanging could be conducted so quietly. The only sound heard during the night was that of McBain fleeing from imaginary pursuers. Sometime before midnight some person was heard to open the door to the pool room in which McBain was confined and whisper hoarsely, 'They're hanging Joe to a telephone pole. Run, Gordon, run like hell.'

"McBain needed no second bidding. He made a bee-line for the mill gulch, the pounding of his iron-shod boots making ghostly thunder in the narrow canyon. It is generally supposed that he is still running. If so, he would be somewhere about Mexico by this time, which is certainly rough on Mexico. He was seen the following morning passing Stovepipe Wells in Death Valley, at a dog trot, a little lame in the near rear hind fetlock . . .

"Local gunmen are already in a chastened frame of mind. Would-be bad men as they bowl along the road on their triumphal entry of Skidoo will note the number, the stoutness, the great convenience of the telephone poles, and reflect thereon. It is a matter of deep regret, but it was the will of the people."

What the editor of the *Skidoo News* did not print was the story behind the story; that Joe 'Hootch' Simpson had to be crazy when he attempted the armed robbery of the bank demanding only twenty dollars. No sane person would rob a bank for a measly twenty dollars. And why did the citizens of Skidoo let him murder Jim Arnold. The newspaper completely ignored the second lynching of old "Hootch". Maybe it was just as well for it was pretty gruesome, even though it was a bigger story than the first lynching.

Wireless telegraphy, which Guglielmo Marconi had invented, had nothing on the desert grapevine when it came to transmitting news in a hurry. In no time the tragic news spread over Harrisburg Flat, causing a general exodus of the miners to Skidoo.

Pete and McNalty rode into Skidoo at dusk. Arnold had just died. As the crowd thickened, there was strong talk of staging a necktie party at once. However, a few level-headed people who were sober, Pete and McNalty being in that category, argued against it, advising the people to let the law take its course. They knew, as did most everyone in Skidoo, that "Hootch" was under the influence of narcotics, for he was suffering from what was then an incurable disease (syphilis) which was destroying the bone structure in the frontal part of his skull. The only way he could stand the constant pain was to stay drunk or under the influence of narcotics.

Dr. MacDonald, who had knelt in the dirt with a rifle aimed at "Hootch" immediately after the murder, had for some time been administering narcotics to him to relieve his suffering. He, above all, knew the terrible condition "Hootch" was in, and that sooner or later, his mind might snap under the strain and he could become dangerous, for he should have been put away before this happened. However, in those days most mining camp inhabitants were rugged individuals who were not prone to meddle in other people's affairs. Consequently, a person could raise all kinds of hell, even live on the shady side of the law, and get away with it, as long as they didn't infringe on other people's rights. The law abiding citizens usually drew the line at murder, rape, horse thievery and claim jumping. There was a standing joke that the county sheriff would never make a trip into Death Valley country for anything less than murder.

Those in the minority who pleaded with the mob to let the law take its course, based their plea on the fact that "Hootch" was out of his mind and did not know what he was doing, and that when he was first disarmed he should have been arrested and taken immediately to the county jail at Independence. The logic of their plea stayed the hand of the mob for three days. However, by the third night the mob had worked itself into such a frenzy, with much alcoholic help, that nothing could stop it.

For the lack of a jail building, "Hootch" had been locked in a stout tool shed for three days and he had been denied alcohol and narcotics. So, in the middle of the night when the mob dragged him out, he was either unconscious or dead. In the ensuing confusion nobody bothered to find out. When the noose of the rope was slipped over his head and he was strung up on the telephone pole, he was beyond knowing what was happening to him.

The next day when his body was cut down and after the shortest inquest on record, he was buried not in the Skidoo boothill, but in a shallow ravine on the opposite side of town.

When the news of the murder and lynching leaked to the outside, the metropolitan press in Reno, San Francisco and Los Angeles sent reporters and photographers to Skidoo to get a first hand story. One thing they didn't reckon with was the transportation problems the newsmen would encounter in reaching Skidoo. They had to travel by standard-gauge and narrow-gauge railroad, by horse-drawn stage, buckboard, horseback, and some of them even had to walk the last few miles. Consequently, when they did reach Skidoo, "Hootch" had been dead and buried for two days.

One would think that when the bully reporters and photographers reached Skidoo, and found that all the excitement was over, they would have been dismayed. They may have been, but not for long, as they set out building a new story.

Never under estimate the ingenuity of the press. The newsmen reaching the scene at Skidoo were not about to spend their papers' money in making the long hard trip into Death Valley country and return to the city without a good story and pictures. So, with much alcoholic help (free drinks) they induced the rough element of the camp to exhume "Hootch's" body, dust it off and re-hang it for the benefit of the photographers. Out of consideration for the women and children in camp, the second hanging was staged in a tent, as you see by the picture elsewhere in this book.

"Hootch" wasn't afforded the decency of a second burial. The ruffians were in a hurry to get back to the newsmen's free drinks in the saloons, so they tossed his body into an abandoned mine shaft.

The Skidoo boom was simmering down at the time and Dr. MacDonald having time on his hands, decided to perform an autopsy on "Hootch's" skull to see how much inroad the disease had made on the bone structure. Using ropes on a dark night, he lowered himself into the mine shaft, and beheaded the corpse! He said it took three days to boil the flesh from the skull.

A year later when the mines petered out, Skidoo was abandoned and it became a ghost town practically over night. Due to the terrific expense of moving one's possessions, it was cheaper to leave them behind. Only that which could be carried handily in a suitcase or trunk was taken. Dr. MacDonald left "Hootch's" skull hidden in his two-room cabin clinic.

Perhaps you would be interested in knowing how the author acquired "Hootch's" skull; it's quite a story. Dr. Homer R. Evans came to Trona in 1914. He was the borax company's first medical doctor. All the old-time prospectors and miners in the area were his friends as he never charged them for their calls. He traded them medical service for their desert relics, consequently he acquired an outstanding collection.

Several years after Skidoo folded, two Trona men, who at times had been patients of Dr. Evans, were drinking at the Hollenbeck Hotel Bar in Los Angeles. They struck up an acquaintance with a heavily bearded man at the bar, who turned out to be Dr. MacDonald, formerly of Randsburg and Skidoo. In the course of their conversation, Dr. Evans and his collection of desert relics were mentioned.

Dr. MacDonald told the men about "Hootch's" skull and where it could be found, and asked them to tell Dr. Evans that he was welcome to add the skull to his collection, if he cared to go after it. In those days it was a long hard trip from Trona to Skidoo.

When the two men returned to Trona and told Dr. Evans about the skull, the good doctor talked them into going after it for him. Sure enough, they found it exactly where Dr. MacDonald said it would be. Dr. MacDonald had hidden the skull in an ore sample bag, suspended from beneath a trap door in the floor of the cabin. The trap door was concealed by a throw rug.

For years the skull adorned the shelf in the waiting room of Dr. Evan's clinic on Panamint Street in Trona. When a patient opened the door to enter the waiting room, the first thing that greeted him was old "Hootch's" skull grinning down from the shelf. I know for sure that it did not boost an ill person's morale. When Dr. Evans retired in 1934, he moved to San Bernardino. In March of 1948, when he heard that I was collecting desert relics, which we had on display at Wildrose Station in the Death Valley National Monument, he gave me several of his relics. Among the choice ones was a pair of ox shoes and a bullet mold, that had been found at the site where the Jayhawkers burned their wagons on Salt Creek in Death Valley in the winter of 1849-50, and old "Hootch's" skull.

It might interest you to know that the mine shaft was not the final resting place of "Hootch". Two "ladies of the night" in Beatty, Nevada—former saloon friends of "Hootch"—upon hearing about his body reposing at the bottom of a mine shaft, decided to give him a decent burial in a legitimate Nevada boot hill. Hiring a wagon and team with an Indian driver, they set out across Death Valley for Skidoo.

Arriving in Skidoo, the Indian went down in the mine shaft and wrapped the corpse in canvas, securely lashed it with rope and hoisted it to the surface. Loading the corpse on the wagon, the funeral party departed for Beatty. It was extremely hot at the time, and somewhere in Death Valley they were forced to abandon the corpse. Returning to Beatty empty handed, they were reluctant to talk about the ordeal except to say that somewhere in the hot sand they had buried "Old Hootch".

Many years later a tourist in Death Valley found some human bones that had been uncovered by the wind in the sand dunes. Who knows? They could have been "Hootch's" bones.

CHAPTER XV

CELEBRATIONS

Skidoo had its brighter side, and except in the case of Joe "Hootch" Simpson and an occasional bar-room brawl, the camp was orderly and peaceful. Sometimes it got a little wild at the Fourth of July celebration. Differences of opinion were settled with the manly art of fisticuffs, and not with guns and knives as they were in tough old Panamint City twenty miles to the south. Panamint City had the reputation of being the wildest and toughest mining camp, not only in California, but in the entire West.

Fourth of July was a big day in Skidoo. All business houses closed except the saloons. The dull thud of the stamps in the gold mill were silent. The miners laid aside their tools to join the celebration. The day of fun was usually opened by a roughly garbed silver-tongued miner, perhaps an ex-lawyer, who would orate elegantly on the patriotism of our forefathers.

His speech was followed by a rock drilling contest and many athletic events. There were foot races, horse races, and hell raising. The latter was brought about by hot beer, hot whiskey and hot tempers. Pete was always a contestant in the foot races for he was an excellent runner, in fact he was the champion foot racer of Skidoo. Every year he won the races he entered. That is, all but one which he lost due to foul play.

Pete had quite a following. Still, there were some who were envious of him, so much so that they would go to the trouble and expense of importing ringers trying to beat him. They would always back their contestants with the content of their purse and never had any trouble getting their bets covered.

The track used for the races was the dusty dirt road which was the main thoroughfare through the camp. The spectators lined both sides of the road and in their excitement of cheering for their favorite, would crowd onto the road. The committee in charge of the races had their hands full in trying to keep them off the track.

There was the time when Pete was racing against a tough man, who was pushing him to the limit to win. Nearing the tape, Pete was leading by a scant two yards, when one of the spectators, who, with the others, was crowding the edge of the track, stuck out his foot and tripped Pete. The judges did not see it and ruled that Pete had fallen and had lost the race.

Pete took a hard fall, sprawling in the dust. He did not see the person who tripped him, but when he got up, the first person he saw was Captain Fleece. The Captain laughed at the wrong time and Pete, before he was dragged away, bopped him on the nose a couple of times, something he had been wanting to do for a long time. The incident caused several fist fights and a free-for-all was narrowly averted.

Pete took pride in his swiftness of foot and he kept in good condition by running great distances. One man probably owed his life to Pete's ability to run many miles in the heat. On a hot summer day Pete was a passenger aboard Jim Calloway's stage enroute from Ballarat to Skidoo. In the middle of Panamint Valley, one of the passengers, a young fellow, suffered a heat stroke and slumped unconscious in his seat.

The driver stopped the team and went to procure water from the keg which was strapped on the rear of the stage. The water keg was empty. He had forgotten to check it before leaving Ballarat, an unpardonable error in the desert.

It was the general opinion among the passengers that the young fellow would die before the stage reached the nearest water at Wildrose Spring. Pete told them that he could beat the stage to the station and that he would meet them on the way back with the water. He took off and ran to Wildrose Spring where he picked up a canteen of water and ran back, meeting the stage three miles below the spring. The stricken man was revived by the water.

There were times when Skidoo was revived on a small scale when leasers worked the old mines. Down through the years there was a lot of mining activity in the surrounding area and the miners continued to hold their Fourth of July celebrations at

Skidoo. Pete ran, and won the race in Skidoo in 1913 and then retired upon his laurels as the undefeated champion of the famous old mining camp.

Pete was nearing forty years of age at the time. He felt that he was too old to race any more and he let it be known that he did not intend to enter the 1914 Fourth of July races.

Two young men, who were studying to be mining engineers at the University of California, were spending their vacation in a practical way, furthering their education by working in a Skidoo mine. They were both track men and were entered in the races. At the insistance of his miner friends, who wanted a miner in the race, Pete came out of retirement and entered the 220-yard dash.

When the contestants toed the mark awaiting the starter's gun, the two California men were clad in track suits and track shoes. Oddly contrasted was Pete, clad in bib overalls and sock feet. The two track men were crouched in the modern fashion with their hands on the ground and their tails in the air. Pete was standing, bent slightly forward with one hand on his knee. At the crack of the starter's gun the track men were off to a flying start, several yards ahead of Pete, but he caught them at the 200-yard mark and passed them in the last 20 yards of the race. The University track men probably wondered for a long time about a 39-year-old man clad in overalls and barefooted beating them.

While Pete was the champion runner, Minnie, a Panamint Indian squaw, who was known as the "Pride of Skidoo", was the champion jockey. Needless to say, she was very popular in Skidoo, especially with the miners. She owned and rode a rangy pinto, which could outrun the best horses in the area. For several years it was a foregone conclusion that Minnie would win the Fourth of July sweepstake, and she did. Minnie's one weakness was fire-water and usually by race time she was "well oiled up". Everybody said the higher she got the faster she rode. But, there came a Fourth of July celebration when Minnie was too high. One drink too many spelled her doom, for in the heat of the race she fell from the horse and broke her neck. Minnie went to the happy hunting grounds quite suddenly.

The Basque are great sportsmen, also there's nothing they like better than attending a festival of some kind. Whenever there was a sports event or a celebration someplace, Pete usually attended, even though it meant riding many tiresome miles.

On September 14, 1907, he, along with Frank Flynn, Billy Pollen and a man named Robertson, went from Harrisburg to Rhyolite to attend a three-day celebration heralding the completion of the Las Vegas and Tonopah Railroad into Rhyolite. The event sponsored by the L.V.&T.R.R. was in celebration of having beat Borax Smith's Tonopah and Tidewater Railroad into Rhyolite.

Borax Smith was frantically building his line north from a junction with the Santa Fe Railroad at Ludlow, California. One amusing incident could have in a small way contributed to his defeat. His construction superintendent, Jim Ryan, a fiery Irishman, ordered a turning plow to be shipped from the Company's refinery at Alameda. After waiting several days for the plow to arrive, he finally received a cow. Imagine a cow in Death Valley and imagine the Irishman's language when the cow arrived.

On July 4, 1910, Pete attended the Jim Jeffries-Jack Johnson heavyweight championship fight in Reno. He had a ring side seat and was sitting next to ex-heavyweight champion Jim Corbett. Corbett was strenuously rooting for Jeffries. He kept jumping to his feet and yelling, "You got him. Kill the S.O.B." Jeffries was taking a terrific licking and near the end of the fight, when he was ready to fold and while in a clinch, Johnson backed him against the ropes above Corbett. Looking over Jeffries' shoulder at Corbett, he patted Jeffries on the back and said to Corbett, "He's mine, and when I polish him off, you can step into the ring big-boy and I'll polish you off too."

The Wednesday, February 7, 1910, edition of the *Los Angeles Examiner* carried a three-column front page story with a picture of one E. Oscar Hart, who called himself the "Chief of the Coyotes". The picture showed the "Chief" surrounded by a large crowd of people who were grasping for the stuff he was throwing away. The "Chief" was nonchalantly tearing hundred dollar bills in half and scattering them along Broadway. Pete was there as a guests of the "Chief" and how he came to be there is a good story.

E. Oscar Hart arrived in Harrisburg one day, representing himself as an eastern multi-millionaire. He was there, so he said, to buy, lease or option mining property; also, he said that he would build a ten stamp mill. When he got around to Pete's property his offer was $150,000 of which $35,000 would immediately be put into escrow to bind the deal. To impress the mine and claim owners with his wealth and sincerity, he invited them to attend a big banquet and champagne party at the Lankershim Hotel in Los Angeles. He also rented, for the night, the swankiest bawdy house in the city for their pleasure. The party was a howling success as it lasted all night and far into the following day.

Pete must have been the honored guest, for the next morning he was singled out to go for a ride in an open air cab with the "Chief". The "Chief" ordered the cabbie to take them to the largest department store in the city. When they alighted from the cab, the "Chief" told the driver to wait. He then began the biggest and craziest spending spree on record at the time. By the time he returned to the hotel a few hours later he had spent $6,000.

Standing at the entrance of the store was a girl selling tiny bunches of violets for a dime. The "Chief" produced a roll of greenbacks that would have choked a horse and gave her a ten spot for a bouquet and told her to keep the change. Entering the store, they almost collided with a woman who was a disciple of Carrie Nation, as she carried the proverbial hatchet. Right away the "Chief" wanted to buy the hatchet. The woman told him it wasn't for sale, but he bought it anyway. Thrusting a ten dollar bill in her hand he took the hatchet. The startled woman, looked at Pete as much as if to ask, "Is the man crazy?" Pete was beginning to think so himself, or maybe it was the champagne jag he was still on.

The "Chief" called for the best suit of clothes in the house for Pete, but Pete refused to accept it. He was wearing a good suit of clothes and one suit was enough for him. He was determined to buy something for Pete, so he jerked his necktie off and said, "Now you need a new tie." He bought him a bright red tie and a fancy stickpin that sparkled in the sunlight. Pete was so mad he wanted to hit the "Chief", but everyone was watching them and he thought he had better not.

News of the man who paid ten dollars for a small bouquet of violets traveled quickly, so when they reached the street, it seemed that every flower vender in town awaited him. The "Chief" didn't disappoint them as he started buying, paying five and ten dollars a bunch. They got to coming so fast that he would buy them by the basket and toss the basket and flowers in the back of the cab. Pete, sitting in the cab, was half covered with flowers.

To escape the crowd the "Chief" climbed into the cab, stepping up on the back seat and began throwing the money to them. Some of the bills he tore in half. When a bill would flutter back in the cab, Pete, like a fool, in place of keeping it, would toss it out. He tossed out a hundred dollar bill and two old gray-haired ladies got hold of one. Neither would let go. They started pulling hair. During the fight the bill was torn in half, so neither profitted by their greed.

Pete began having a feeling that the man's crazy actions were going to cost him something in the end, and it did. About the time the "Chief's" money played out, the crowd had grown so large that traffic was completely blocked. The street car motormen were clanging their bells, but to no avail. Finally, the cops came and cleared the street. When the first streetcar passed, the "Chief" jumped from the cab and caught the car on the run, leaving Pete and the driver holding the bag with a carload of flowers. After the "Chief's" sudden departure, the crowd, still clamoring for money, thought that Pete should take his turn playing Santa Claus. Some of the vendors who had been paid a hundred times the value of their flowers and baskets, which the "Chief" had tossed into the cab, were insisting that Pete pay them again for the baskets. Pete was about to be mobbed from all sides when the cops came to his rescue. Dispersing the crowd, they told the cabbie to drive on or they would run them both in.

Returning to the Lankershim Hotel, Pete paid the cab bill. Entering the hotel bar, there stood the "Chief", having a drink and smiling as though it was all a big joke. Pete was so angry he could hardly see, but what was a poor desert man to do in a situation like this where a supposed multi-millionaire was involved? The "Chief's" greeting was, "Hello, Pete, have a drink." Later, when they left the bar, the "Chief" was reduced to a few silver coins. When they reached the street, with a "whoopee" he tossed the remaining coins in the air.

The next morning the "Chief of the Coyotes" caught a train for New York, leaving an unpaid hotel bill of $400 with the Lankershim Hotel. In trying to balance the books, Pete found that his debits consisted of his fare to Los Angeles, the "Chief's" cab fare, the loss of the sale of his mine and a headache. While his credits consisted of a swell time at the party, a red necktie and a fancy stickpin that the barbers always admired.

CHAPTER XVI

BEAR TALE

If you had asked Death Valley Scotty, when he was living, if there were bear in the Panamint Mountains, he would have said, "Why shore." If you had asked him if he could prove it, his answer would have been, "Well, I reckon I should know as I killed a big one at Harrisburg Flat in 1910."

What Scotty wouldn't have told you though, was that after he killed the bear, Harrisburg Flat wasn't a safe place for him to visit for a long time as Pete Aguereberry was gunning for him. Scotty had killed Pete's pet bear and thereby hangs a bear tale.

Pete neglected to chain the bear up one day when he went away. That night, when he came home, the bear wasn't around, nor did it come when he called. Next morning he started a search and found his pet dead, victim of a gunshot wound. What Death Valley Scotty wouldn't have told you was, that the bear he killed in the Panamint Mountains was dragging a chain.

Domingo Etcharren, a fellow Basque, owned a cattle ranch between Darwin and Coso Hot Springs. In the summer time, he ranged his cattle in the Monache Meadows, high in the Sierra Nevada Mountains west of Olancha. Whenever Pete could get away from his mine, he would assist Domingo, working as a cowboy, with the spring drive and the fall roundup.

In the fall of 1908 Pete was riding along looking for strays in Gomez Meadow, when he encountered a "she bear" in close quarters. The only firearm Pete packed was a .32 caliber revolver. The other cowboys all packed .45's and they were always kidding Pete about his toy pistol, asking him what he would do if he met a bear. If the cowboys had been around when he met the bear, he would have shown them what he could do with his toy gun. Without dismounting, he shot the bear. The bear went down but got up immediately and charged. The horse wheeled so quickly that it fell to its knees. With the bear almost on top of them, he fired twice more. Luckily one bullet pierced the heart and the bear died instantly.

Tying one end of his lariat around the bear's hind paws and the other end to the saddle horn, he dragged it to the nearest tree and hung it from a limb. When he returned to the cow camp and told the boys that he had killed a bear with his toy gun, they wouldn't believe him. The next morning when he caught a pack mule and started back to get the bear, no one would go along to help load the bear on the mule. Being alone he had to skin the bear and cut the carcass in half in order to load it on the mule. He had snubbed the mule up close to a tree but hadn't blindfolded it, so when he attempted to load it, the mule wheeled and kicked a mighty blow; fortunately the mule kicked the half of the bear that Pete was holding in his arms. The force of the blow sent Pete and the bear meat sprawling. Not until he blindfolded the mule was he able to load it.

Riding into camp that evening with his bear, Pete was most welcome as the cowboys welcomed a change of meat after having been on a steady diet of beef all fall. They also quit kidding Pete about his toy gun.

Pete was told that a "she" bear would only attack a human to protect her cub and that if he didn't go back and find the cub it would starve to death. He rode back the next day, and sure enough, when he neared the vicinity, he heard the hungry cub squalling for its mama.

When the cub saw Pete it scampered up in a tree. He climbed up after it. The cub went out on the end of a limb just out of reach. Descending, Pete got his rope and lassoed it. When the cub hit the ground it slipped the noose and high-tailed it out across the meadow. Pete mounted his horse, rode it down and lassoed it again. Wrapping it in a blanket he placed it on the saddle in front of him and started for camp.

The poor little cub was crying like a baby and struggling to free itself. Tearing a hole in the blanket with its sharp claws it bit clear through Pete's finger and clawed the horse, causing them both to be bucked off. Finally he got the cub into camp and tied it to a tree, but before doing so he weighed it. It weighed seventeen pounds. (When Scotty killed it, it weighed 350 pounds.)

One day when all the cowboys were out working with the cattle and the camp was vacated, the cub broke loose and got in the cook's sour dough which had been placed in the sun to rise. That evening when they came in, they found dough all over everything, but most of it was on the cub. When the cub saw Pete, it climbed a tree where it remained for the night.

When the roundup was over and the cattle driven from the mountains, they made camp one night in Olancha. Some of the cowboys were Indians and they got hold of enough firewater to make them want to go on the warpath. They wanted to scalp something, so their interest centered on the bear cub. Pete was aroused from slumber in time to prevent the act, by scalping the ring leader with the butt of his gun.

One of Pete's favorite stories about Death Valley Scotty had to do with how he promoted publicity. Once, when Pete was a guest at the Hollenbeck Hotel in Los Angeles, he unexpectedly met Scotty in the lobby. Scotty was in a jovial mood and his greetings were, "Hello Pete. What are you doing out of the Panamints?" Pete told him that he was in town on mining business. Scotty invited him to have a drink. Going into the hotel bar the price of the two drinks was fifty cents which Scotty paid for with a hundred dollar bill. When Pete ordered a round of drinks, Scotty cancelled the order, saying let's go to another bar. When they got outside they went across the street to a bank, where Scotty added a fifty-cent piece to the $99.50 change the Hollenbeck bartender had returned to him, and requested a hundred dollar bill from the bank teller. They made every saloon in the vicinity buying one round of drinks and in between drinks they would return to the bank where Scotty would pony up an extra fifty cents and get another hundred dollar bill. Pete thought that Scotty was crazy, that is, until he saw the headlines in the morning newspaper: "DEATH VALLEY SCOTTY IN TOWN SPENDING $100 BILLS."

Yes! Scotty knew how to get publicity all right.

CHAPTER XVII

SAM ADAMS

The obituary of Sam Adams read like this: "Stove Pipe Wells (Death Valley) March 12, 1930—Sam Adams, Death Valley's oldest prospector, has heard the last call. He died at the home of a friend, Mrs. Sam Newman, in Los Angeles, at the age of 83 years. Sam, who lived alone in a shack adjoining his mining claim in Wildrose Canyon, had boasted that he never had known a sick day, and only a few weeks before he died he chuckled that he could do a bigger day's work with the pick and shovel than many a younger man.

"Mrs. Newman, who had known the octogenarian prospector for many years, had exacted a promise from his partners that if the old man should ever get sick they would bring him to her home. So, a week ago they tenderly brought him down to the big city, knowing that Sam was nearing the last call.

"Sam Adams was born October 22, 1847, in Indiana. He came to California in 1885 and began prospecting in Death Valley country where he became identified as one of its outstanding desert characters. Wherever there was a big strike, Sam was sure to be there. Despite the fact that he had lived in the border towns during their wildest and bloodiest days, Sam Adams prided himself in that he never took a drink of whiskey or 'toted a gun.' Sam did not believe in violence. After the infamous lynching in Skidoo in 1908, the one and only telephone pole mysteriously disappeared. Only recently did Sam admit with a chuckle that he pulled the pole down and burned it so that there could be no more lynchings.

"At one time a pair of desperados who heard Sam had made a rich strike, tried to follow him. Sam frightened them away by poking his corncob pipe through his coat pocket.

"Not long ago, Sam Adams returned to Death Valley on the stage from a trip to Los Angeles. With a canteen slung over his back, to the dismay of fellow passengers, he got off along the road and started alone on a 17-mile trek across uncharted wastes for his cabin in Wildrose.

"Sam Adams had a keen sense of humor and in later years enjoyed regaling tourists with yarns of wild prospecting days when, with his faithful burro, he wandered the desert wasteland. His partners, Bill Corcoran, Charlie Walker and John Cyte, Shorty Harris and Dad Fairbanks mourn Sam Adams. It is expected that he will be buried somewhere in the desert he so loved."

Whoever wrote Sam Adams' obituary, did not know Sam very well or else they were giving him the benefit of the doubt. But there was no doubt in the minds of the old-timers about the kind of man Sam Adams was. He was a man addicted to strong drink and he had a violent temper. As Dr. Homer Evans would have said about the obituary, "What a lot of bull." The late Jack Stewart, renowned desert philosopher, had a pet expression for Sam: "That guy was as phony as a nine dollar bill." This is the way they knew Sam Adams and the stories they told about him:

When Sam arrived in California in 1885, he settled in Los Angeles where eventually he became a small-time politician, a ward worker, sometimes called ward heeler. About the time Pete Aguereberry discovered gold at Harrisburg, Los Angeles had become unhealthy for Sam, so he came to Harrisburg, which had just begun to boom, and established a store and a saloon in a large tent. Sam was cunning. He was also a braggart and he never passed up an opportunity to extol his political exploits to the bar patrons.

The "Blue Sky" mining promoters infested the new mining camps like fleas on a dog. They were, as a whole, a breed to be shunned, as their word was nil and their credit rating was lower than a snake's belly. Working on a shoestring they were usually just one jump behind the big deal they were always going to promote, and often times they were actually hungry. In Sam they found a person with whom to match chicanery, and in doing so were able to fill their stomachs. Their mode of operation worked this way. A couple of their members would saunter up to the bar and, while dallying over a drink, would engage Sam in his favorite conversation, politics. Sam would become so deeply involved in the subject that he was oblivious to all things material, making it easy for their henchmen to lift the canvas at the rear of the tent and filch Sam's canned food.

Sam Adams wasn't long in Death Valley country until he began to dabble in politics. He got himself appointed deputy sheriff and then began to give the boys a bad time. Sam had brought to Harrisburg and Skidoo, the petty, chiseling crookedness of the Los Angeles political era of the 80's and 90's, which was a mistake on his part. He just didn't understand the desert men or their code of ethics. A desert man was as good as his word and ninety-eight percent of them lived up to the expectation.

You may have noticed that Pete Aguereberry and Sam Ball were not listed among the mourners in Sam Adams' obituary. It was just as well that they were not mentioned for they wouldn't have liked it a bit. They had no use for Sam Adams; to them he was a trouble-maker who had dealt them plenty of misery, especially to Pete.

Sam Ball was a typical desert rat, who wasn't too particular about personal cleanliness. His white beard was usually stained with tobacco juice, as was the front of his shirt. The lower button on his shirt was invariably missing and so was the top button of his pants. Consequently, a patch of his long-handled underwear was always exposed. Sam didn't mind if you didn't. Strangely, his cabin was always clean and the latch-string was always out to the wayfarer, even when he was out in the hills prospecting or out of the country. The door to his cabin was never locked. Anyone passing by was welcome to go in and cook a meal. There was only one thing Sam expected out of them, they had better wash the dishes.

Sam Ball's trouble with Sam Adams happened after prohibition came into being and the country was legally dry. Ball was the moonshiner and town bootlegger at Skidoo, and Adams, the deputy sheriff, was his best customer; that is, his best non-paying customer. Before embarking upon the illicit profession, Ball made a deal with Adams. If the latter would let him operate, he would keep him supplied with free liquor.

Adams was short, stocky and barrel chested, weighing in the neighborhood of two-hundred pounds. He consumed a lot of liquor. He was a silent drinker and he could drink as much as the average two men without visible effect. This Ball knew since he was furnishing the liquor.

It must be said that during the period of prohibition, the sheriff's office at Independence was tolerant about the flow of booze in the far out-of-the-way places, such as Death Valley country. Wise in the ways of hard working men, they knew that the hardy miners who manned the mines had to have some kind of diversion and drinking hard liquor was one of them. If they couldn't go on a spree occasionally, they were liable to brain each other.

The sheriff's office knew that trying to stop a miner from drinking or procuring liquor would be as ineffectual as trying to stop the flow of time. So, they merely winked at what was going on in the isolated mining camps. Normally they only intervened when violence occurred, such as murder.

This was the case in Skidoo when Sam Ball almost killed Sam Adams by whacking him on the back of the neck with a length of tool steel. It happened when Adams committed the unpardonable sin of the desert. He broke his word with Ball. Ball was faithfully keeping his word by giving Adams whiskey in return for protection, when one day "Ornery Adams" strode into Ball's cabin and declared, "You are under arrest."

Startled Ball asked, "What for?"

"Bootlegging," Adams replied.

Adams didn't have to look for the evidence. He knew where it was, for hadn't he helped himself many times to the cache of liquor concealed under a trap door in the floor of the cabin? When Adams stooped over to lift the trap door, Ball let him have it. Adams went down like a polled hog and shuddered like one in the agony of death. Ball thought that he had killed him, but no such luck, as Adams was too rugged an individual. However, he was unable to walk for a week, much less make an arrest.

Eventually, Ball was arrested and taken to Independence. When he told his story at the preliminary hearing, the judge fined him thirty dollars and turned him loose. Shortly afterwards, Adams' deputyship terminated suddenly. Then, when an election was held in Skidoo to fill the office of constable, by popular choice Sam Ball was elected.

With the end of the boom at Harrisburg Flat, Sam Adams closed his tent store and moved to Skidoo. With the decline of Skidoo, he moved back to the Flat where he built a cabin on the north rim some two miles distant from Pete's cabin and mine. When settled in his new home, he turned his attention to Pete, which led to a long and bitter feud. The trouble started when he appropriated Pete's blacksmith tools without telling him.

There was an unwritten agreement among desert mining men. To borrow tools and equipment from each other, regardless of whether the owner is at home or not, the borrower must know that the tools or equipment he takes are not being used by the owner at the time and he must leave a note stating what he borrowed or send word to the owner. In Pete's case he was using his blacksmith tools, and when they turned up missing, he was unable to find a note, nor did anyone volunteer information that he had borrowed them. Pete's search for the tools was rewarded when he found them at Sam Adams' place. Hot words were exchanged as Pete retrieved the tools. From that day hence, animosity began to build up between the two miners. Sam seemed to take the offense, so Pete thought, for he became the butt of some mysterious happenings that were annoying and expensive.

Pete was never able to pin a thing on Sam, but he strongly suspected him. The feud reached a climax at Wildrose Spring, when Sam attempted to kill Pete with an axe, but we are getting ahead of the story.

Many times in the dead of night, Pete would be awakened from deep slumber by thrown stones rattling on the tin roof of his cabin. Grabbing his gun he would go searching in the darkness for the miscreant, but he was never able to catch him.

Late one night Pete was riding his horse from Skidoo. As he neared his cabin, it burst into flame. Riding hard he attempted to reach the cabin in time to save his trunk which contained valuable papers, old pictures, $600 in currency and several gold buttons. But, when he reached the cabin, the fire had gained so much headway, he was unable to save anything. Knowing he had twenty pounds of giant powder and several barrels of gasoline stored in the shed adjoining the cabin and several rounds of ammunition in the cabin, he retreated to what he thought was a safe distance, awaiting the explosion. The cartridges exploded first and a shell case fragment hit him, embedding in his hand. The powder and drums of gasoline exploded with a terrific roar, spreading fire over a sizeable area of Harrisburg Flat. To top it all off, his horse stampeded and ran away, leaving him stranded in the darkness with the ashes of his cabin, and injured.

While Pete was having his misfortunes, other strange things were happening in the district. There was only one route into Skidoo, a narrow treacherous road that wound around the rim of the mountain. Near the top a huge boulder hung precariously over the road. With the help of a soft charge of powder the giant boulder toppled onto the road one night. Skidoo was isolated until the boulder was blasted away. John Burns had filed on the water at Emigrant Spring and decided to build a custom gold mill. At great expense he had lumber freighted in. One night the lumber went up in smoke. Upon investigating, Burns found strange tracks around where the lumber had been burned. He hired Indian Tom Wilson to follow the tracks. Tom tracked the man for forty miles into Ballarat. Enroute, the man he was tracking changed boots. Sam Adams was in Ballarat with an extra pair of boots.

The Aguereberry-Adams feud reached its climax at the old Wildrose Spring. A cloudburst had taken the canyon road out and, as this road was the only exit to the west for the miners of the Wildrose Mining District, the road had to be rebuilt as quickly as possible. A crew of miners and mine owners went to work on the road for the county. Adams, due to his political connections, was in charge of the work. It was his duty to sign the county pay warrants. Pete worked eighteen days on the road and when he went to Adams for his warrant, Adams said that he had only worked fifteen days and he signed a warrant for that amount of work.

When Pete refused to accept the warrant, a bitter argument ensued in which Pete called Adams a crook. Adams grabbed an axe and made for Pete. Pete took off down the canyon. Adams, with the axe held above his head, was in hot pursuit. Bill Stevens, another member of the road crew, caught Adams from behind, pinioned his arms and took the axe away from him.

Pete and Adams were now on equal footing and they staged one of the bloodiest fights in the history of the Panamints. Both powerful men, tough and hardened, as only miners can be, asked no quarters nor did they give any. Adams had a thirty pound weight advantage, but Pete was younger by several years. With the members of the road crew as spectators they fought it out to a finish.

Pete unleashed a cyclonic attack upon Adams that carried all the pent-up hatred that had been generating for years. His first blow knocked Adams down. Shaking off the effects of the blow, Adams held his ground, giving as good as he received, but then Pete's youth began to tell and he slowly wore Adams down. Hammering away, he beat him to his knees and kept pounding away until Adams went down and out. The fight had ended for unconscious Adams.

Utterly exhausted, bruised and bleeding, Pete sat down heavily alongside Adams. When he was able, he extracted a blank warrant from Adams' pocket and filled it out for eighteen days work. When Adams regained consciousness, Pete thrust the warrant and a pencil in his hand, saying, "Now will you sign this warrant for eighteen days work?" Adams answered, "I can't sign it, Pete. You have closed both my eyes." Pete guided his hand and he signed the warrant.

Adams—bruised, bloody and disheveled—crossed the San Bernardino County line into Trona where he tried to swear out a warrant for Pete's arrest. The Trona constable told him that the matter was out of his jurisdiction and that he would have to file the complaint in Inyo County. He also told him that Pete Aguereberry should be awarded a medal for a good deed well done.

Adams headed out of Trona for Independence. Two days later he stopped at Chappo Romero's roadhouse at Olancha wearing the same clothes, with dried blood still caked on him because he hadn't washed. Mrs. Romero offered to wash and dress his injuries, but he wouldn't let her, for he wanted to look as bad as possible when he presented his complaint to the sheriff.

Arriving in Independence, he told Sheriff Frank Logan and Jesse Hession, the district attorney, that the crazy Frenchman, Pete Aguereberry had tried to kill him. They agreed with him that, by his looks, someone had tried to kill him, but, before taking any action, they would have to investigate the matter.

Logan and Hession went to Harrisburg, had lunch with Pete and heard his side of the story. Before they departed they present-

ed him with a box of cigars. On their way home they stopped at
Lonnie Lee's General Store in Darwin where they encountered
Sam Adams, whose clothing was still caked with dried blood.
When Adams learned that they hadn't arrested Pete, he blew up
a storm, creating such a disturbance that they arrested him and
took him to Independence and placed him under a peace bond.

A short time after Adams returned to Harrisburg Flat, Pete
found his saddle horse shot to death near Adams' cabin.

CHAPTER XVIII

JEANE (JOHN) LeMOIGNE

The now famous Jeane (John) LeMoigne, a brave prospector and miner, died with his boots on in Death Valley. LeMoigne was well-met, through his willingness to help his fellow men, he had a host of friends throughout the Death Valley country.

He discovered and opened the LeMoigne Silver Mine at the extreme north end of the Panamint Mountains in Cottonwood Canyon. Also, he discovered lead in what is known today as LeMoigne Canyon northwest of Emigrant Spring. LeMoigne's silver mine could have been the "Lost Gunsight Lode" that a segment of the '49er emigrants discovered, but could never find again.

Pete and LeMoigne were good friends and neighbors, as they lived only twenty miles apart, which was close for neighbors in that rugged country. They were fellow countrymen, Frenchmen, and whenever they got together they reminisced in their native tongue about their life in the old country. One day, LeMoigne—tired, dirty and hungry—stumbled into Pete's camp carrying a gallon jug which contained about two fingers of whiskey. His pockets were weighed down with chunks of practically pure silver. As he wolfed down the meal Pete prepared, he told how the silver was found.

He had been visiting friends in Panamint City and as a parting gift they gave him a gallon of whiskey. It was summertime and to avoid the heat in Panamint Valley, he stuck to the high country on his way home. Following the Indian trail that led up and over the Panamints down Johnson Canyon to Hungry Bill's ranch and on into Death Valley, he turned north at the summit of the mountain but the contour was too rugged for travel, so he dropped back down away and skirted the crown of Telescope Peak to

133

the west. As the going got rougher through schist, shale and blind canyons he began to lighten his load by partaking of the contents of the jug of whiskey.

Many miles and many drinks from Panamint City, as he was working through an extremely rough stretch, following a narrow ledge along a canyon wall, the ledge gave way beneath him and he fell several feet. He managed to hold on to the whiskey jug and miraculously it wasn't broken. At the end of the fall he landed in a sitting position and around him were several chunks of gleaming silver. Looking up, he saw that the silver had come from the ledge that had caused his fall. The ledge was about two feet thick and at least a hundred feet long. After making a mental picture of the location of the ledge and filling his pockets with chunks of silver, he headed for Pete's place which was on his route home. He told Pete that his discovery would be another Panamint City, maybe larger.

LeMoigne could never retrace his steps to the rich ledge. He and Pete spent many months searching for the lost treasure without success. The old desert and its mountains had a way of deceiving and hiding its wealth from even the ablest of the old-time prospectors. It could have been that the contents of the jug had some bearing on LeMoigne not being able to find the ledge again, or it could have been that a flash cloudburst covered the ledge up again as neatly as it might have uncovered it; who knows?

In the early spring of 1918 Pete took Mac McCarty, the superintendent of the Copper Queen mine to investigate LeMoigne's lead property in LeMoigne Canyon. They found LeMoigne camped at Emigrant Spring. He was about out of grub and broke. Before leaving, McCarty gave him what food they had left and Pete gave him $75. LeMoigne didn't want to accept the food and money as he was a proud old man, but they talked him into taking it by telling him that he could pay them later.

Pete never saw LeMoigne again for in June of that year, Death Valley Scotty found LeMoigne's body, along with his three burros, south of Salt Creek hills in Death Valley.

In the long ago the Trona Borax Company had a narrow gauge railroad whose lone train would have compared favorably with Fontaine Fox's famous "Toonerville Trolly" cartoons. There was some difference though. The Trona train's engine was gasoline powered and it pulled a string of small dump cars that hauled trona from the east side of Searles Lake into the plant.

The railroad was affectionally called the "Mexican Central" by the local people inasmuch as it hauled the Mexican laborers who harvested the trona to and from the lake. Oscar "Swede" Johnson, who came to work for the Borax Company in 1911 and stayed to become one of the town's beloved old-timers, was, at the time of our story, a one-man crew on the "Mexican Central". Oscar served as engineer, conductor, brakeman and porter, and, if the track needed repairing, he could do that too.

The Copper Queen Mine (later renamed "Goldbottom") is located in the Slate Range Mountains directly across the lake from the town of Trona. The mine's mill was located near the east shore of Searles Lake and the Mexican Central hauled freight (hay, grain and mining supplies) across the lake for the Copper Queen.

During World War I in 1918, Pete tried to enlist in the U.S. Army, but was rejected as physically unfit. Doing the next best thing for the war effort, he went to mining lead at the Copper Queen, lead being a strategic mineral. Oscar Johnson and Pete were good friends. When Pete came down out of the Panamints, Oscar hauled him and his bedroll across the lake on the "Mexican Central" to his new job at the Copper Queen Mine.

The Copper Queen was a dusty, dangerous mine. The operators cared little for the miners' safety and health welfare. Consequently most of the miners, if they stayed on the job long enough, contracted arsenic poisoning, lead poisoning, or fell victim to an accident. Pete was no exception. In due time he had a touch of arsenic poisoning, and he became leaded. This slowed him down so much that he couldn't get out of the way of a falling boulder which broke his leg.

D.W. "Pop" Whipple, a native of Steamboat Springs, Colorado, who went on to become a prominent mining man in the Searles Lake country, was hired by the Copper Queen to act as Pete's nurse while he was convalescing in the company bunkhouse.

When Pete was able to use crutches, he went to Coso Hot Springs to finish recuperating. At Coso he met Tom Kirk, a friend of his from Tonopah and Goldfield days. Kirk had been drafted in the army and was killing time at the health resort awaiting induction. Their reunion was short-lived. Two days after Pete's arrival, Kirk took a natural steam bath in one of the caves, and, without spending the prescribed time in the cooling room, he exposed himself to the chilly weather. The next day he was dead, a victim of double pneumonia. Kirk's brother was an undertaker in Bishop, California, and he came down and picked up his brother's body.

While Pete was there, the terrible World War I influenza epidemic hit Coso and the people died like flies. Four died in one day. The county (Inyo) had to bury most of the victims and the coffins were built on the spot. Pete contracted the disease and became critically ill. From his cabin he could hear the noise of hammering and sawing as the coffins were being made. By raising his head at times he could look out the window and watch the operation. The coffins were stood on end in a row when the carpenters completed them. As Pete viewed the coffins he wondered which one he would occupy. Eventually he recovered sufficiently to go to Trona where he fell victim to pneumonia.

Thanks to a rugged constitution, Pete survived the following ailments and accidents in succession: arsenic and lead poisoning, a broken leg, influenza and pneumonia. The people in the Panamints didn't think so though, since a rumor spread like wildfire throughout the region that Pete had died in Trona and had been buried there.

For a long time Shorty Harris had coveted four of Pete's good silver claims in the Panamints. When he heard the sad news about Pete, he high-tailed it to the mountains and jumped the claims. The manner in which he jumped the claims was crudely done. He merely scratched Pete's name off the location notices, inserted his name and changed the date. It was several months later, when Pete went to do the assessment work on the claims, that he discovered Shorty's chicanery. Shorty was out of the country at the time, but Pete knew that sooner or later he would show up and, when he did, he would work the short man over.

The meeting occurred at Wildrose Spring. Pete went down for water and found Shorty camped there with Bobby Taylor and Charley Grundy. When Shorty saw Pete, despite his desert tan, he turned pale and started stuttering, "Why, why, why, Pete, I thought you were dead."

"I am dead," was Pete's reply. "You are looking at a ghost and you are going to have the distinction of being the first person to have the hell beat out of him by a ghost." With these words he let Shorty have it, knocking him down. Shorty had never been hit by a ghost before and it sure hurt. Pete hauled him to his feet, and with his fist cocked, said, "Shorty, I'm going to break you from claim jumping." He let him have it again. The ghost kept picking Shorty up and knocking him down until Taylor and Grundy intervened. As they dragged Pete away, Grundy said, "We know that Shorty had it coming, but you have punished him enough. Now let him be." Afterwards, whenever Shorty met Pete, he gave him a wide berth.

What had happened in Trona was that, when Pete had recovered from his seige with pneumonia and was able to work again, he had been buried, so to speak, in Homewood Canyon. "Pop" Whipple and Henry Scheffnet were partners in some mining claims on which they had built a cabin in the canyon. They hired Pete to do the assessment work. "Pop" drove up to the claims and told him that he would find plenty of food in the cabin and then drove away. All the grub Pete found was some hard biscuits and peach jam. A week later when "Pop" came back, Pete greeted him by saying, "Meester Whipple, if you expect me to complete the job, you will have to provide me with meat, beans and potatoes, something that will stick to my ribs."

Pete bought his first automobile from Hardee Witt in Randsburg in 1920. It was a used "Model-T Ford". Having been a sheepherder, burro herder and horseman, he knew nothing about the mechanism of an automobile or how to drive one. A friend of his in Johannesburg attempted to teach him how to drive on the wide open spaces of the baseball park. Pete was 46-years-old at the time and trying to teach him to drive was like trying to teach an old dog new tricks. When a man reaches middle-age and has never driven a car, he never learns to drive, he only learns to herd one. So it was with Pete, he never learned to be a good driver. But he could surely herd a car in a hurry on the wrong side of the road around treacherous curves on a narrow mountain roadway.

Frenchmen believe in getting all the speed there is out of an automobile, regardless of what's in the way or how dangerous the road may be. Pete was no exception. Believe me, I know, for once —and only once—I rode with him and I was never so scared in my life. We were going from his home at Harrisburg Flat down the mountain to Wildrose Station. At the start of the ride, Pete tramped the accelerator to the floor board and we took off with a jerk amidst the noise of screeching tires and flying gravel. Sometimes we were on two wheels and, when we hit dips, we weren't on any—we were flying through the air! He straightened out all the mountain curves on the wrong side of the road and occasionally he complained that the motor wasn't running good. Hanging on for dear life, I was praying that the motor would conk out completely. I still shudder when I think about that ride.

How he ever drove the first Model-T Ford safely over the Slate Range crossing was a mystery to me. God must have had his arms around him. It wasn't until 1932 that he had his first bad wreck. He blamed the wind for upsetting the car. He was on his way to Shoshone to see Supervisor Charley Brown. Clipping along in Death Valley, he failed to make a curve. The car rolled over three times and came to rest upside down, trapping him in the car. When he regained consciousness from his upside-down position the only thing he could see was blood and ashes. The ashes had come from the pipe he had been smoking.

A short time before, at the Trona airport on Searles Lake, he had helped remove the body of an ex-World War I German flier ace, whose plane had crashed from a distance of several hundred feet. The cowling of the plane had been spattered with the pilot's brains. Pete had had a good look at the brains, and now, as he gazed at the blood and ashes, he wondered if they were his brains, for it sure looked like them. That was Pete's story and he always enjoyed telling it. The late Father Crowley used the story in his column "Sage and Tumbleweeds," which appeared in the *Inyo-Independent* newspaper.

There wasn't much travel in Death Valley in those days, so Pete was trapped in the wreck for a long time. When he was found, he was taken to Death Valley Junction where he was patched up at the Pacific Coast Borax Clinic. Fortunately, he wasn't seriously hurt. Harry Gower, who was general manager of the Borax Company at the time, had Pete's car towed in and repaired free of charge in the company garage.

CHAPTER XIX

ARNAUD AGUEREBERRY

On the morning of July 19, 1933, two French Basques entered the Trona Food Market. They were seeking direction and information about the Aguereberry Mine at Harrisburg Flat. Someone directed them to the writer who was employed in the market at the time. Introductions revealed them to be Arnaud Aguereberry, who was Pete's brother, and Ambroise Aguereberry, his nephew. They were on their way to visit Pete.

The writer was pleased to meet them, especially Arnaud, for he had heard Pete speak of him many times. Arnaud had come from France in 1884 and was living in San Francisco when Pete arrived in 1890, as described earlier. Pete idolized his older brother, for it was he who took Pete under his wing and helped him establish himself in this new and strange country. After giving them the desired road information and a brief chat, the two Aguereberry's went on their way. Little did the writer suspect that before night, Arnaud would be dead.

Ambroise, who was driving the car, did not follow the instructions given him. He became lost and wound up far to the west in Darwin Wash, many miles from Harrisburg Flat. The day was extremely hot, much too hot for Arnaud who lived in a much cooler climate at San Pedro on the coast. They met someone in Darwin Wash who directed them to Harrisburg Flat. While driving through Wildrose Canyon, Arnaud heaved a sigh and died, a victim of fatigue and the desert heat. He remained sitting upright in the car. Ambroise knew that his uncle was dead, but there was nothing he could do but drive on to Pete's home at the mine.

Darkness had fallen when he arrived. Uncle Pete wasn't home, but from the appearance of the place, he felt that his uncle wasn't far away and he should return shortly. Completely exhausted, Ambroise collapsed on a bench in front of the cabin and passed out. Pete was visiting his nearest neighbor, Silent George Greist, sheriff of the Panamints, who lived at the Argenta Mine in Wood Canyon. It was two o'clock in the morning when Pete returned home and found the strange car parked in front of the cabin. He wondered who it could be. As he approached the car, he saw the faint outline of a man sitting on the front seat. He spoke three times and was not answered, so he lit a match. As the flame flared he recognized his brother. When he took hold of his brother's arm to awaken him, the arm was cold and stiff and he knew that his brother was dead. Pete wasn't expecting a visit from his brother and the shock of finding him dead in the darkness caused him to have a slight heart attack.

From this point on Pete was never a well man. In 1938, Ambroise, his nephew, came to live with him and to help with the work in the mine. This was a boon to Pete as he wasn't physically able to do the hard work. Ambroise had come from Los Angeles where he had worked as a waiter in high-class French cafes. From life and laughter to the solitude of the towering Panamints was a new world for him. He knew nothing about the art of mining, but Uncle Pete was a good teacher and he was willing to learn.

Until near the end of his life, Pete continued to guide people through his mine and up the mountain to "Aguereberry Point" where on a clear day one could see for hundreds of miles. Pete usually began his talk by saying, "Folks, you're looking 6,000 feet straight down, be careful and don't fall off." He would then tell them that Death Valley was 140 miles long, six to 15-miles wide and from Aguereberry Point they could see it all. He would then point out Blackwater Canyon, practically at their feet to the south, through which he and Shorty Harris punched their burros in 1905. Away to the northwest was Mt. Whitney (14,496 ft.) the highest point in the continental United States. And, to the southeast at the very bottom of Death Valley, there was Badwater, 282 feet below sea level, the lowest spot in the western hemisphere. (Mt. Whitney and Badwater are only 80 miles apart and both are in Inyo County.)

Pete had a sense of humor and he usually finished the tour with a story. One he told that never failed to draw a laugh was about a Swedish miner. "Back in the early days when he had a crew of men mining, they all slept in the same tent. Among them was a big Swede who was a heavy drinker. A trade rat was invading their quarters at night, while the men were asleep, and was trading sticks for objects that it could pack away—like silver coins, watches, rings, keys and 'snoose' cans. The men set a big rat trap for the culprit. Late one night the Swede awoke with the usual hangover and, while blundering around in the dark searching for water, he stepped on the trap, which caught his big toe with painful pressure. The Swede woke everybody up. Hopping around on one foot, yelling, "Yumping yimminy, yumping yimminy! Gila monster! Take him off!"

Pete had a lot of desert relics. There were two that he valued highly, a pitcher pump and a hand wrought trace chain. He found the pump and chain in Death Valley in 1907 at the site on Salt Creek where the "Jayhawkers" burned their wagons in the winter of 1849-50. After Ambroise came to live with him, Pete was away one day when a scrap iron buyer came to the mine. Ambroise sold all the scrap iron around the place, including the emigrant pump and chain for $18.00.

High-grading and highwaymen came simultaneously to the Death Valley country, when in April 1873, R.C. Jacobs, R.B. Stewart and W.L. Kennedy discovered rich silver at Panamint City. The fabulous rich mines coupled with its isolation and hard accessibility attracted a motley crew of desperadoes, most of whom had a price on their heads. A few of the bad men staked claims that turned into rich mines. They sold their bullion to local buyers in Panamint City and, when it was shipped out, they would go part way down Surprise Canyon, hold up and rob the stages and freight wagon of the bullion, and then sell it again.

When the heat was put on, the desperadoes were forced to sell their mines. The sale was usually made through a middleman. In one instance when a sale was made and the payoff came in San Francisco, a freight line company stepped in and demanded $12,000 to cover losses due to hijacking of its treasure box in Surprise Canyon by the party selling the mine. In this case, the party concerned was given his choice of making the payment or going to jail. He paid and boldly asked for a receipt in full.

Contrary to popular belief, Wells Fargo stages did not run

in to Panamint City. They contracted their treasure hauling business to other stage and freight lines. When Nevada Senators Bill Stewart and John P. Jones acquired most of the mines at Panamint City, they solved the problem of shipping the bullion safely, by moulding it into quarter ton balls.

The major high-grading of the Panamint City era, has dwindled down through the years to more recent times. A ton or two of good ore will be stolen while the owner is away and the mine and mill machinery will be carted away from an unattended mine. An example or two of how it is carried on: a crew of men were working at a mine in the Panamints. They knocked off work for a few days and went into town for the usual spree. A couple of the miners had business elsewhere, so they said, and after the rest of the crew departed, they backed a truck up to the mine, loaded the hoist, engine, cable and ore bucket and hauled the equipment to Nevada, where they had a pre-arranged sale. Then, they returned to the mine with the rest of the crew and discovered the theft. The two culprits were the most surprised of all.

On Easter Sunday in 1939, Pete and Ambroise attended Sunrise Service, conducted by Father John J. Crowley at the sand dunes in Death Valley. When they returned home, they found that a ton and a half of hand-picked high-grade ore had been trucked away. Even on Easter they steal.

High-grading and hijacking was not confined alone to rich ore and valuable mining equipment. Even the whiskey runners were waylaid and robbed. During prohibition, Ash Meadows, located east of Death Valley Junction just across the Nevada line, was a haven for moonshiners. This was due to the abundance of good artesian water and laxity of the law. Ash Meadows whiskey was better than most (it must have been the water) and it brought a premium price. It sold for $12 a gallon in Trona.

Bob Weir, operating out of Homewood Canyon, was one of Searles Valley's prominent bootleggers. He handled Ash Meadows whiskey exclusively. Bob, a rugged Scotchman, had once been a miner until he found an easier way of making a living. He and Pete were friends as they had once mined together. One night, when Bob was running three barrels of Ash Meadows whiskey across Death Valley, he was ambushed in Emigrant Wash. By knowing the roads well and being able to turn the truck lights off as it wasn't too dark a night, he managed to escape through a hail of bullets. The hijackers gave chase and when Bob reached the Aguereberry turnoff in Harrisburg Flat, he whipped off the main road and around the hill up to the mine. Enlisting Pete's aid they managed to save the whiskey by hiding it in a mine tunnel.

CHAPTER XX

PETE'S LEGACY

Pete's health failed rapidly in 1943, and by 1944 he was in pretty bad shape. We had been after him for a long time, trying to pursuade him to go to a good clinic or hospital for a thorough examination and treatment. He was reluctant to go, as he never had much faith in the medical profession. It was not until he reached the point that he was walking almost bent double that he consented to go. Sadly, he packed his bag and went down to Loma Linda, where he entered the hospital. At the end of a week he was back. When questioned, he was bitter. He hadn't liked the place because there was too much noise, right next to a railroad. They wouldn't let him smoke and they had hidden his pants so that he couldn't leave until they were through with him. They told him that he had "silicosis". This he already knew, as he had had it for years. Silicosis, an occupational disease, was prevalent among the early-day miners and stonecutters, caused by breathing rock dust which settles in the lungs. The old-timers, many of whom died of the disease, had a pet name for it. They called it "rocks in the box."

One thing Pete did learn at Loma Linda was that the "thing" in his stomach which he called a "knot" was a growing tumor, and that it should be removed immediately. On March 1, 1944 the tumor was successfully removed at the Santa Fe Hospital in Los Angeles. Pete recuperated from the operation in San Pedro at the home of his sister-in-law, Arnaud Aguereberry's widow.

When Pete finally decided to have the operation, the trip to Los Angeles was made in three stages. On the second leg of the trip, if it hadn't been for the timely intervention of the writer, Pete would probably have eliminated himself and Charley Nunn from the face of the earth in a motel unit at Panamint Springs.

144

In late February, my family and I, along with our partner Charley Nunn, spent a three-day weekend at Wildrose Station which we then owned. It rained constantly the three days we were there. On the second day Pete came down from Harrisburg Flat, where it was snowing. (Harrisburg is the only place where I have heard it snowing. The snowflakes, as large as half-dollars, were wet and heavy and when they struck the ground the sound they made was plop, plop, plop.) He was to leave his pickup truck at Wildrose Station and ride in to Trona with us, where he would take the stage to Los Angeles. Late Sunday afternoon when we were preparing to leave for Trona, we discovered we had three flat tires on our Buick. The air had slowly leaked out of the tubes, which had been pinched by small breaks in the tires, which were caused by sharp rocks in the rough dirt roads.

The tires could only be inflated to fifteen pounds each as there was insufficient air pressure in the tank. Due to the prolonged dampness, we couldn't start the one-lunger gasoline engine which powered the air compressor. We were anxious to get out of the canyon as water was already running on the road. So, we took off in an overloaded car, with three half-inflated tires which were leaking slowly. It was forty miles to Trona, and we figured we'd never make it, so we headed for Panamint Springs which was only seventeen miles away.

That was the longest seventeen miles I have ever driven. It was done mostly in low gear. Panamint Valley was covered with water in many places and there were times when I had to guess where the road was. At times the front end of the car dropped into ditches of running water and I would wonder if it was going out of sight, but it always came up and we kept grinding along. Finally, we made it to Highway 190 and turned west toward Panamint Springs.

At the time, the Panamint Springs resort was operated by the original owners, Bill and Agnes Reid. The Reids were pioneer talc miners in the Darwin country. I was to get up the next morning at six o'clock and help Bill fix our flat tires. Bill was recovering from a heart attack and wasn't supposed to do any manual labor. When I arose at daylight, it was bitter cold. All the mountains surrounding Panamint Valley were blanketed with snow. I went to wake up Pete and Charley who were sharing a motel unit. Rapping on the door, I was told to come in and when I opened the door a strong gust of Butane blew by me. There sat Pete in his long-handled underwear in front of the unlit and unvented gas heater. He had a match in one hand and a cigarette in the other, and was just in the act of striking the match when I rushed in and knocked it from his hand. I remember saying, "My gosh, Pete! What are you trying to do. Blow yourself up?" He said, "I opened the valve a little bit and no flame come. So, I opened it some more, and no flame come. So, I opened it wide open and still no flame come." I told him that if he had struck the match, the flame would have come, enough to blow him to kingdom come. Pete wasn't accustomed to gas, he was a woodburning man. Charley Nunn, with the bed covers pulled over his head, slept peacefully through all the commotion.

The sudden death of Pete Aguereberry on November 23, 1945 at Tecopa Hot Springs wasn't too much of a shock to his many friends as he had been ailing for several years. The shock came later when they learned the details of his death. His body was found floating face down in the spring in which he had been bathing.

A few weeks before his death, he had been confined to the Trona Hospital and when he was discharged, he had gone to Tecopa to recuperate. Tecopa is a small, isolated community located ten miles south of Shoshone and east of the southern end of Death Valley. Three days had elapsed before the news of his death reached Trona.

Pete is buried in the Mt. Whitney Cemetery at Lone Pine, California. The pallbearers at his funeral were: Ralph Merritt, Clark Mills, Ranger Sam Huston, John Thorndike, Oscar Johnson and the author.

On that cold November morning in 1945, we sat in the Santa Rosa Catholic Church in Lone Pine and listened to the Memorial Mass being said by Father Fred Crowley, who was the brother of the beloved Desert Padre, Monsignor John J. Crowley. As the good Father spoke on and on, my thoughts were of many things and I was glad that I could record Pete's life for posterity. I knew that I, and many people in the Death Valley country, had lost a dear friend and the world had lost a good man.

I thought of how fast the old-timers were going, passing into the great beyond—Pete's friends and my friends. Chris Wicht was gone and so were Ed McSperrin, Dan Driscoll, Bob Warnack, Sam Ball, Carl Mengel, Jim Sherlock, Chris Tyler, John Oven, Harry Hughes, Indian George Hansen and many others. Now in the casket before me lay my friend Pete Aguereberry. I thought of a religious incident that Helen Gunn had told me about Pete. This was Helen's story:

During Father John J. Crowley's visits to Death Valley to say Mass at Death Valley Junction, Furnace Creek Inn and at the Civilian Conservation Camp on Cow Creek, he many times drove to Pete's home at Harrisburg Flat where he spent the night and said Mass the following morning before going on his way. Pete, who had served as an alter boy in France, served the altar for Father Crowley, remembering the Latin responses. Pete had not been to confession in forty years. Father Crowley would talk to him about it, and ask him to come to confession and Holy Communion. Pete always promised that he would.

The summer after Father Crowley was so tragically killed in an automobile accident, Pete went to visit Helen Gunn for a week at her home in Independence. While he was there, he told her of his promise to Father Crowley, and he asked her to help prepare him for the confession. Helen invited Father Maginis, a Jesuit Priest in Mono County for the summer, to come to her home and talk to Pete, which he did. She also invited Father Smith, the pastor of the Santa Rosa Church, to dinner one night. After the meal she retired leaving the Father and Pete to discuss Pete's going to confession. They decided on Sunday morning, before the early Mass, at 7:30. Pete was up and dressed at 5:30 waiting to go. Helen and he started about six as he was anxious to be there early.

They waited in the church until Father Smith came in the confessional at 7:00. Then Pete made his confession. During the Mass, Helen and he went to Holy Communion and when Pete left the altar railing and returned to his seat, he faced the altar and said, "Father Crowley, I have kept my promise to you." All who heard were touched by his sincerity.

After we lowered Pete into the grave and after the last words were said by Father Crowley, I humbly bowed my head and thought "Au Revoir, Pete. You are gone but not forgotten, for as long as there is a Death Valley National Monument, people will stand on Aguereberry Point and glory in the handiwork of God. The beauty of the view was part of your religion which you unselfishly shared with your fellow man."

Pete had said many times that he wanted to be buried on the Point he discovered, built a road to and which bears his name. The directors of the National Park Service deemed otherwise.

ABOUT *the* AUTHOR

George Cook Pipkin was born on September 19, 1902, in Pine Bluff, Arkansas (the home of Martha Mitchell who blew the whistle on the Watergate scandal). Pine Bluff was named by Daniel Boone, who, while seeking to trade with the Indians, paddled a canoe up the Arkansas River through a hundred miles of swamp land from the Mississippi River. Rounding a sweeping bend in the river he came upon a high bluff covered with pine trees. Here the swamp ended and here Daniel found a tribe of Indians with whom to do business. The city of Pine Bluff grew out of the trading post he established there.

It is said that the "Arkies" and the "Okies" took the State of California without firing a shot. The invasion came during the great depression and the dust bowl days of the 1930s. Pipkin was twenty years ahead of the main invasion. When he was a small boy of nine years, his father Albert Henry Pipkin brought him west for his health. Fourteen months of roaming the hills in the dry desert country of the western San Joaquin Valley oil fields, near the town of Coalinga, restored Pipkin's health.

Returning to Arkansas he was enrolled in school and went on to attend schools in Houston, Texas and Oklahoma City before having to quit school to go to work. Much to his credit, he is a self-educated man.

Pipkin had California in his blood and he longed to live there. So at the age of 21 and married, he shook the dust of Arkansas from his feet and returned to the Golden State. The time was April, 1923. After spending eight months in Los Angeles he moved to the desert in 1924, where he was employed by the Inyo Chemical Company at Cartago, California, on the shore of Owens

Lake in southern Inyo County. Pipkin operated the company store and ice plant and for a time was acting postmaster.

While at Cartago he played on the baseball team which was a member of the Owens Valley Sunday League. This league consisted of seven teams: Cartago, Keeler, Ash Creek, Lone Pine, Independence and two teams in Bishop, one of which was an Indian team.

In April, 1928, Pipkin moved to Trona where he worked for American Potash and Chemical Corporation for 31 years between 1928-46 and 1953-67. Pipkin's ability as a ball player had some bearing on obtaining the job in Trona. The Company sponsored the crack "Trona Tigers" team, and bore the expense of bringing up good semi-pro teams from Southern California to play Sunday games for the entertainment of their employees, who were more or less isolated at the end of the railroad on the fringe of the Death Valley country.

As a player, and eight years later as the team manager, Pipkin wrote a sports column for the Company weekly newspaper, the *Trona Potash*. He was also the sports editor of the paper for a period of time. In 1943 the name of the newspaper was changed to the *Trona Argonaut* and Pipkin wrote an historical column entitled "Desert Sands". In 1963 he published *Desert Sands*, a book of desert short stories which went into a second printing in 1964.

The first edition of the Pete Aguereberry story was published in 1971. A book entitled *Ballarat Facts and Folklore*, co-authored by Pipkin, Paul B. Hubbard and Doris Bray, was published in 1965 and had a second printing in 1972. This was a story of the famous ghost town, Ballarat, in Panamint Valley.

Pipkin now resides in Renton, Washington, with his wife, Bernice.

INDEX

Adams, Sam, 67, 90, 125-132

Aguereberry, Ambroise, 139-142

Aguereberry, Arnaud, 16, 22-23, 36, 95, 139

Aguereberry, Jean Pierre "Pete",
Aguereberry-Adams Feud, 129-132
American Citizenship, 43
Assessment work, 95, 105
Burros, 25, 53, 56-57, 62, 64, 66-67, 69-70, 73-75, 79, 85-89, 94-95, 100, 140
Cashier's check ($100,000), 10
Chestnut Harvest, 16
Childhood, 15
Convalescence, 28-29
Crossing Death Valley (summer), 57-61
Dairyman, 36-37
Death of Mother, 38-39
Death of Pete, 12, 136, 146-147
Eureka Mining Claims, 10, 70, 74, 88, 90, 93, 99-101, 105
Fight with Sinclair, 48-49
First job, 23
"Fooling the Ewe", 33
Foot racing, 26-27, 115-117
Fourth of July, 9, 69-71, 73, 115-117
French Basque, 10, 15
"French Pete", 15, 69, 72, 86
Gambler, 49-50, 106
Gold strike (Eureka Mine), 70, 74
"Greenie", 19, 50, 62
Grubstakers, 9, 53, 84-85, 88, 91-95
Handball player, 23-24
Harrisburg/Harrisberry, 73, 75

Haying crew, 38
Ice deliveryman, 48
Influenza Epidemic, 136
Injuries, 16-17, 22, 24, 27-29, 103, 135
Journey to America, 15, 17-20
Language(s), 10, 34-35, 68
Litigation, 91-96, 100
Miner, 10, 40, 48
Mineral springs curative powers, 12, 104
Money exchange, 19
Napolean claim, 100
Pet Bear, 122-124
Pneumonia, 45, 136
Prospector, 9, 52
Ranch hand, 10, 36
Rosa, 41-42, 44
Sheep dog, 32-33
Sheepherder, 10, 23-25, 30-35, 44-45, 78
Shooting by Crawford, 103-104
Silicosis, 144
Skunk escapade, 37
Sour wine, 22
Stage driver, 37-38, 45
Trail partner, 11
Water hauler, 48

Aguereberry, Papa (Pete's Father), 15, 17

Aguereberry Point, 9, 11, 13, 71, 140, 148

Alameda (Calif.), 118

Aldrich, Sherwood, 53, 91-95

Alpine County (Calif.), 32

Amargosa Desert, 12, 80

Amargosa River, 53
America, 15-16, 18, 36, 44
American Potash & Chemical
    Corporation, 11
Anthony Mine, 79
Argenta Mine, 140
Argus (Calif.), 80
Argus Mountains, 79
Arnold, Jim, 107-109, 111
Ash Meadows (Nev.), 100, 142
Atlantic Ocean, 20
Austin (Nev.), 47
Australia, 79

Badwater (lowest point in USA), 140
Bah-vanda-sava-nu-ke (Indian George
    Hansen), 78
Bakersfield (Calif.), 31, 64
Ball, Sam, 127-128, 147
Ballarat (Calif.), 9, 11, 53, 55, 66,
    68-72, 74-76, 79-85, 87, 89-90, 100,
    105, 116, 130
Barnum, P. T., 64
Barstow (Calif.), 92
Basque(s), 12, 16-19, 23-24, 28, 31,
    34, 35, 41, 42, 58, 71, 81, 94, 117,
    122, 139
    Emigrants, 16-17, 20
Beatty (Nev.), 53, 114
Beatty Ranch, 53, 56
Belgium, 31
Bennett-Arcane Party, 65
Bennett Wells, 63, 77-78
Big Flat (Panamints), 76
Birch Spring, 99
Bishop (Calif.), 51, 136
Black Mountains, 67
Blackwater Canyon, 9, 69, 85, 140
Bodge, Charles Emory, 107
"Bohemian", 110
Booth (Surveyor), 52-53
Borax Mining in Death Valley, 62-63
Borax Smith, 62, 118
Bordeaux (France), 17-18
Borden, Shorty, 81

Bottle House (Rhyolite, Nev.), 55
Bower Saloon (Tonopah, Nev.), 49
Boyles, Jim, 77
Bridgeport (Calif.), 35
Brougher, Wilson, 48
Brown, Charley (Supervisor, Inyo
    County, Board of), 138
Bullfrog District (Nev.), 53, 54, 72,
    74, 75
Bullfrog-Goldfield RR., 54
Burns, John, 130
Butler, Jim (Prosecutor, Nye County,
    Nev.), 47
Butte (Montana), 67
Byrne (prospector), 67

CCC, see Civilian Conservation Corps.
California, 15, 16-17, 20, 31, 35, 41
Calloway
    Hotel (in Ballarat), 80, 101
    Jack, 81
    Jim, 80, 116
    Lester, 81
Candelaria (Nev.), 48
Cantill, Shorty, 52
Cape Horn, 80
Caricart, John, 81
"Cashier" Claims (Shorty Harris), 99
Cattlemen, 34
Chalfant, W. A.,
    (Death Valley—The Facts), 63
Chateau (French ship), 18
Cherry Creek (Nev.), 44
Chicago (Ill.), 65
"Chief of the Coyotes", 118-121
Chinatown (San Francisco), 23
Christian Endeavor Society, 38
Civilian Conservation Corps (and
    camp), the CCC, 147
Clendenning Stage Company, 45
Club Saloon (in Skidoo), 110
Coalinga (Calif.), 31, 33
Coffin Canyon, 64
Connell, Tom, 84
Cook, John S., Company, 55

Cooper (Mine), 79
Copper Queen Mine (Goldbottom), 135
Copper strike (Greenwater, Calif.), 67
Corbett, Jim, 118
Corcoran, Bill, 126
Coso Hot Springs (Calif.), 100, 104, 122. 135-136
Cottonwood Canyon, 133
Cow Creek, CCC Camp, 147
Crawford, Sam, 103-104
Cress, Jack, 81
Cross, Ed, 54
Crowley, Fred (Father), 12, 146
Crowley, John J. (Monsignor), 12, 138, 142, 146-147
Culverwell, Captain (Death Valley emigrant), 65
Cummins, Neil, 81
Cyte, John, 126

Daggett (Calif.), 63
"Dago", 66, 103
Dalton Mine, 40
Darwin (Calif.), 79, 82, 100, 105, 122, 132, 145
Darwin Wash, 139
Daylight Pass, 57
Dayton, James W., 63
Death Valley, 9, 11, 13, 15, 53, 57-61, 62-71, 73, 74, 75, 80, 88, 90, 94, 95, 100, 107, 110, 111, 114, 118, 125-128, 133, 138, 140-142, 146-147
Death Valley emigrants, 65-66, 77-78, 114, 141
Death Valley Gold Mining & Developing Co., 64,
Death Valley Indians, 62, 78, 93, 117, 130, 147
Death Valley Junction (Calif.), 138, 142, 147
Death Valley National Monument, 9, 11, 114, 147
Death Valley Scotty, 64, 122, 124, 134

Death Valley (record temperature), 62, 66
Decker, Richard (Judge at Ballarat), 80
Denton, Oscar, 62, 64-65, 69
Department of Interior, Board of Geographic Names, 10
Dobbs, Ralph E., 107, 108
Driscoll, Dan, 59, 147

Easter Sunday, 142
Echo Canyon, 66, 67
Elko (Nev.), 43, 44
Ely (Nev.), 45
Emigrant Canyon, 69, 78
Emigrant Spring, 60, 74, 78, 88, 89, 93, 98, 106, 130, 133, 134
Emigrant Wash, 60, 93, 98, 99, 142
English (language), 10, 34, 68
Epstine, Ben, 109
Eskimos, 64
Estrem, Edouard & Jean, 31
Etcharren, Domingo, 58, 81, 122
Eureka (Nev.), 45
Eureka Mine, 10, 70, 74, 88, 90, 93, 99-101
Evans, Dr. Homer R., 80, 113-114, 126

Fairbanks, "Dad", 126
Father Fred Crowley, 12, 146
Father John J. Crowley (Monsignor), 12, 138, 142, 146-147
Father Maginis (Jesuit Priest), 147
Father Smith (Pastor, Santa Rosa Church), 147
Ferge, Charles ("Seldom Seen Slim"), 81
First National Bank (Rhyolite, Nev.), 55, 94
Fish Creek (Nev.), 44
Fish (Death Valley emigrant), 65
Flause, Thomas, 107
Fleece, Captain, 91-92, 94-95, 100, 105, 116

Fleece, "Spec", 91, 95, 100, 105
Flynn, Frank, 9, 53, 88, 90-95, 118
Foisie, Joe L., 81
Fontaine, Frank, 134
Ford, Claude, 44
Ford, J.M., (Supervisor, Inyo County, Board of), 44
Forty Mile Canyon, 55-56
Fourth of July, 9, 69-71, 73, 115-117
France, 31
French Basque, *see* Basque(s)
French Liquor Store (Madera, Calif.), 41
"French Pete", 15, 69, 72, 86
Fresno (Calif.), 28, 31
Funeral Mountains, 57, 60, 62, 64, 66
Furnace Creek, 67, 68, 78, 94
Furnace Creek Inn, 67, 147
Furnace Creek Ranch (Greenland Ranch), 9, 60, 62, 66
Furnace Creek Wash, 77

Gayhart, Walter, 47
Glendenning, Mrs. Milly, 106
Golar Canyon, 35
Goldbottom Mine (formerly Copper Queen), 135
Goldfield (Nev.), 9, 51-53, 66, 68, 88, 90, 135
Gold Seal Saloon (in Skidoo), 108
Gold strike, 35
Gomez Meadow, 122
Gotcher, Al, 106
Gower, Harry, 138
Gray, Fred, 80, 90
Greenland Ranch (Furnace Creek Ranch), 9, 60, 62, 76
Greenwater, 53, 67
Greist, "Silent" George, 140
Grundy, Charley, 136-137
Gunn, Helen, 147

Hamilton (Nev.), 45
Hanaupah Canyon, 69
Handball, 23-24

Hanford (Calif.), 24
Hanksite Saloon (Tonopah), 50
Hansen, Indian George, 77, 147
Hawaiian Islands, 87
Harris, Frank "Shorty", 9, 10, 11, 54, 63, 69-75, 82, 84-90, 99, 126, 136-137, 140
Harrisberry, 11, 75, 85, 90
Harrisburg, 11, 66, 67, 71, 75, 85, 90-93, 95, 97, 100-101, 103 104-106, 118, 126, 127, 131, 138
Harrisburg Flat(s), 10-11, 13, 57, 90, 99, 111, 122, 129-130, 132, 138, 139, 143, 147
Hart, E. Oscar, 118
Hession, Jesse (District Attorney, Inyo County), 131
Hicks, Frank (assayer), 47
Hicks (prospector), 66-67
High Sierras, 31, 35, 105, 122
Hollenbeck Hotel (Los Angeles), 91, 95, 113, 124
Holtville (Calif.), 106
Homewood Canyon, 137, 142
Honeybee District, 32
Houston, Sam (National Park Ranger), 146
Hovic, Steve, 98
Hubbard, Paul, 12
Hughes, Harry, 147
Hungry Bill's Ranch, 133
Huron (Calif.), 24-26, 28, 31

Independence (Calif.), 90, 109, 112, 128, 131, 132, 147
Indian country, 20-21
Indian George Hansen, 77
Indian Ranch (Warm Springs, in Panamint Valley), 76-77
Indian Wells Valley, 31
Inyo County (Calif.), 9, 15, 31, 90, 131, 136, 140
Inyo Independent, 138
Irishman (Jim Ryan), 118
Irish miners, 83

Italian, 34, 40
Italian emigrants, 18, 20
Italian Swiss Colony Winery, 41

Jacobs, R. C., 141
Jail Canyon, 99
January Mine, 52
Jawbone Canyon, 32
Jayhawkers Party, 65, 77-78, 114, 141
Jeffries, Jim, 118
Jew, 50-51
Joaquin, Enacio, 76
Johannesburg (Calif.), 79, 80, 82, 92, 100, 137
Johnson Canyon, 69, 133
Johnson, Jack, 118
Johnson, Oscar "Swede", 135, 146
Jones, January, 52
Jones, John P. (Nev. Senator), 141
Jones, O.K. (attorney), 92-95

Kavanagh, Tom, 9, 53, 88, 90-91, 94-95
Keane, Jack, 58
Keane Spring, 58-59
Keane Wonder Mine, 53, 58-59
Kelso Valley, 32
Kennedy, Frank, 72-73, 75, 89-90
Kennedy, Joe, 76
Kennedy, W.L., 141
Kern River Valley, 32
Kerr-McGee Chemical Corporation, 11
Kettleman Hills, 31
Kirk, Tom, 135-136
Klondike Mine (Eureka, Nev.), 48
Kunze, Arthur, 67

Lankershim Hotel (Los Angeles), 119-120
Las Vegas-Tonopah RR., 54, 94, 118
Lee, Lonnie, 82-83, 132
Le Harve (France), 18-19
LeMoigne Canyon, 133-134
LeMoigne, Jean (John), 133-134
Levine (partner of Capt. Fleece), 95

Levit (prospector), 66-67
Lila C. Borate Mine, 80
Logan, Frank (Sheriff), 131
Loma Linda Hospital, 143
Lone Mountain, 51
Lone Pine (Calif.), 12, 83, 146
Los Angeles (Calif.), 21, 65, 85, 91-94, 100, 112, 119, 121, 124, 125, 126, 140, 143, 145
Los Angeles Examiner, 118
Los Banos (Calif.), 31, 42
Lost Gunsight Lode, 133
Ludlow (Calif.), 118

MacDonald, Dr. Reginald E., 80, 108-109, 111, 113, 114
MacDonald, Irish, 23
Madera (Calif.), 36, 40, 44
Maginis, Father, 147
Manly-Bennett Party, 77-78
Marconi, Guglielmo, 111
Mauleon (France), 15-17, 58
Mayflower Mine, 55
McBain, Gordon, 109-110
McCall (partner of Capt. Fleece), 95
McCarty, Mac, 134
McDonald, Ed, 103-104
McKenzie (Aldrich's partner), 92-93
McNalty, Tom, 106, 111
McNamara (Slaughter house owner), 51
McSperrin, Ed, 147
Memorial Mass, 12, 146
Mengel, Carl, 147
Merritt, Ralph, 146
Meyers, Al, 51, 81
"Mexican Central" Railroad, 135
Mexicans, 34
Mexico, 110
Mills, Clark, 66, 146
Minnie ("Pride of Skidoo"), 117
Mining Syndicate, 10
Modesto (Calif.), 30-31
Mojave (Calif.), 31

Molly (Indian George's grand-daughter), 78
Monache Meadows, 32, 122
Mono County (Calif.), 31, 147
Montana, 78
Montezuma (Nev.), 52
Montgomery, Bob, 97-100
Montgomery pipeline (Skidoo), 97-100
Montgomery-Shohone Mine, 97
Moonshiners, 127
Mt. Whitney Cemetery, 12, 146
Mt. Whitney, 140
Murphy, Bill, 55
Murphy, Tom, 52
"Mysterious Scott", 64

NBC television, 81
Nation, Carrie, 119
National Park Service, 148
Navares, Adolph, 53
Negroes, 19-20
Nemo Canyon, 73, 76, 87
New Jersey, 47
New Orleans, 20
Newman, Mrs. Sam, 125
New York City, 19-20, 120
Nunn, Charley, 144-146
Nye County (Nev.), 47

Oak Creek Canyon, 32
Oakes, Fred, 108
Oakland (Calif.), 21, 31
O Be Joyful Mine, 79
Oddie, Tasker (District Attorney, Nye County, Nev.), 47
Olancha (Calif.), 32, 100, 122, 124, 131
Old Indian Ranch, 76-77
Oly Elliot Saloon (Goldfield, Nev.), 52
Oven, John, 147
Owens Valley, 31-32, 103, 105

Pacho, 25
Pacific Coast Borax Clinic, 138

Palisade (Calif.), 45
Pallbearers, 12, 146
Palm Sunday, 12
Palo Alto, Bernard & Pedro, 43
Panamint City (Calif.), 51, 80, 115, 133-134, 141, 142
Panamint Indians, 77, 78, 93, 117
Panamint Mountains, 9, 13, 15, 53, 57, 60, 65-66, 70, 76, 77-78, 79, 94, 97, 105, 122, 124, 130, 133, 135, 140
Panamint Springs, 144-145
Panamint Valley, 79, 116, 133, 145
Paris (France), 18
Pietsch, Henry (Constable), 80
Pinto Peak, 76
Piute Mountains, 32
Pleasant Canyon, 79, 83
Pollen, Billy, 118
Porter Brothers Store (Rhyolite), 55
Poso (Calif.), 31
Price, Dr., 99
Prohibition, 127, 142
Pyreness (France), 15, 16, 22, 25, 31, 38, 58

Ramsey, Harry, 97
Rand District, 35
Randsburg (Calif.), 12, 80, 113, 137
Ratcliff Mine, 79, 83
Raymond (Calif.), 36
Redwood (drive thru) Tree, 36
Reid, Bill & Agnes, 145
Reno (Nev.), 112, 118
Rhyolite Herald, 54
Rhyolite (Nev.), 53, 54, 57, 60, 88, 90-95, 97, 100, 118
Ridgecrest (Calif.), 12
Robertson —, 118
Robinson, Wm. (Death Valley emigrant), 65
Romero, Chappo, 131
Ruby Valley, 53
Ryan, Jim, 118
Ryan, Tim, 61

Sacramento (Calif.), 30, 32
"Sage and Tumbleweeds" (Father John J. Crowley), 138
Salt Creek, 77-78, 114, 134, 141
San Bernardino (Calif.), 114
San Bernardino County, 131
San Francisquito Ranch, 65
San Francisco (Calif.), 10, 16, 21, 23-24, 38, 43, 44, 80, 91, 95, 112, 139, 141
San Francisco Chronicle, 31
San Joaquin Valley, 24, 31-32, 42
San Pedro (Calif.), 10, 139, 143
Santa Fe Hospital (Los Angeles), 143
Santa Fe Railroad, 65, 80, 118
Santa Rosa Catholic Church, 12, 146-147
Scheffnet, Henry, 137
Schwab, Charles M., 67
Scotchman, 142
Scottish widow, 44
Searles Lake, 135, 138
Searles Station (Calif.), 31
Searles Valley, 142
See-umba (Telescope Peak), 77
Seldom Seen Slim (Charles Ferge), 81
Sellers, Henry (deputy sheriff), 108-109
Sharman (at Skidoo), 98
Sheepherding, 10, 23-25, 30-35, 44-45, 78
Sheppard Canyon, 105
Sherlock, Jim, 147
Shoshone (Calif.), 138, 146
Shoshone Indians, 62, 78
Shoshone Johnnie, 93
Sierra Nevada Mountains, 31, 35, 105, 122
Simpson, Joe "Hootch", 99, 106-115
Skeleton Mine, 64
Skidoo (Calif.), 12, 66, 92, 95, 97-101, 104-117, 125, 126, 128-130
Skidoo News (report of "Hootch" Simpson lynching), 107-110, 111
Skidoo Trading Company, 108

Slate Range Mountains, 65, 79, 82, 135, 138
Smith, Borax, 62, 118
Smith (mining engineer), 101
Smith, Father (Pastor Santa Rosa Church), 147
South Fork (Kern River), 32
Southern California Bank (Skidoo), 107-108
Southern Pacific RR., 36
Spain, 17
Spanish, 34
Spanish-American War, 43
Spanish border, 15
Spanish Ranch (Nev.), 43-44
Steamboat Springs (Colo.), 135
Stevens, Bill, 130
Stewart, Bill (Nev. Senator), 142
Stewart, Jack, 126
Stewart, R.B., 141
Stockton (Calif.), 30
Stovepipe Wells, 60, 66, 77, 110, 125
Strike (labor), 11
Summit Diggins, 35
Surprise Canyon, 141
Surveyor Well, 77
Sutherland (Aldrich's partner), 92
Swedish miner, 141
Sweet, Jack, 81

Taylor, Bobby, 136-137
Tecopa Hot Springs (Calif.), 12, 146
Tehachapi (Calif.), 35
Tehachapi Mountains, 31, 32
Telescope Peak, 61, 77, 99, 133
Terry (prospector), 72, 75
Texas, 20
Theisse, Judge, 110
Thompson, "One-eyed", 97
Thorndike, John, 146
Thurman, R.M., 86-88
Tibo, George, 49-50
Tilson, Clarence, 64
Tilton, Frank, 63
Tombstone Flats, 64

Tomesha (ground afire), 57
Tonopah Club, 50
Tonopah (Nev.), 47, 49-51, 67, 135
Tonopah & Tidewater RR., 54, 118
"Toonerville Trolly", 134
Trail Canyon, 69
Trona Borax Company, 134
Trona (Calif.), 10-12, 77, 80, 92, 105,
    113-114, 131, 135-138, 142, 145
Trona Food Market, 139
Trona Hospital, 12, 146
Trona Potash, 12
Tuber Canyon, 76
Tujunga (Calif.), 51
Tuolumne River (Calif.), 30
Tyler, Chris, 147
Tyler, Clair, 81

Ubehebe Crater, 65
Ubner, Julian, 55
Union Station (Rhyolite), 54
United States, 43, 108, 140
United States Dept. of Interior, Board
    of Geographic Names, 10
University of California, 117
U.S. Army, 135
U.S. Bureau of Mines, 105
U.S. Mail, 45

Viewpoint, Aguereberry, 15
Viper, 38-39
Virginia City (Nev.), 48

Wagner, Laura May, 81
Walker, Charlie, 126
Warm Springs, 48-49, 69, 76-77
Warm Springs Canyon, 69
Warnack, Bob, 147
Washburn Stage Line, 36, 38
Weir, Bob, 142
Weldon (Calif.), 32
Wells Fargo Company, 141
Westmoreland, Wes, 55
Whitney, Mt., 140
Wicht, Chris, 79-83, 147
Wildrose (cutoff), 9
Wildrose Canyon, 72, 76, 101, 125,
    126, 139
Wildrose Mining District, 73, 90, 130
Wildrose Spring, 72-73, 75, 76, 85, 87,
    89-90, 116, 129, 130, 136
Wildrose Station, 64, 114, 138, 145
Williams, Ralph, 80
Wilson, Indian Tom, 77, 130
Wipple, D.W. "Pop", 135, 137
Witte, Hardee, 137
Wood Canyon, 70-71, 76, 140

York, E.C., 81-82, 84-85, 88
Yosemite Park, 36, 38
Young (at Keane Wonder Mine), 58

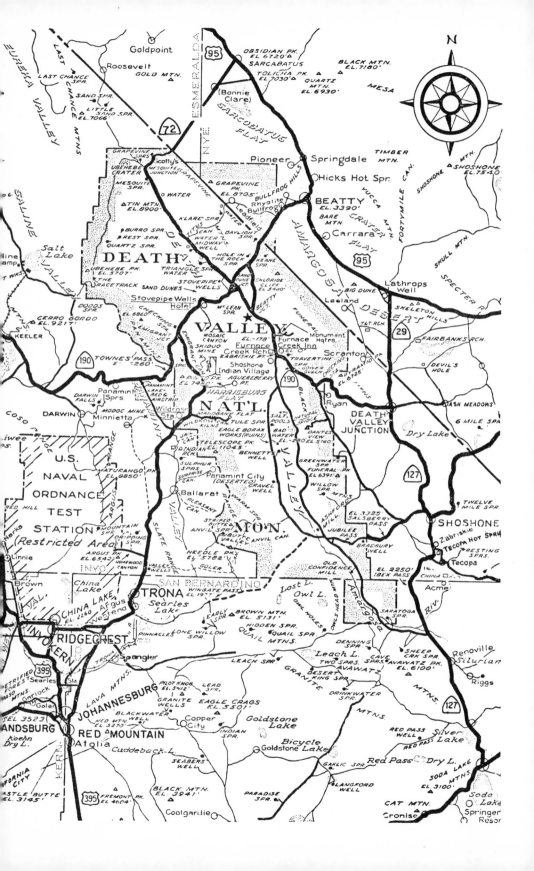